THE IRAQ WAR

A Controversial War in Perspective

Titles in the Issues in Focus Today *series:*

Beyond Bruises
The Truth About Teens and Abuse
ISBN-13: 978-0-7660-3064-0

China in the 21st Century
A New World Power
ISBN-13: 978-0-7660-2684-1

The Evolution Debate
Darwinism vs. Intelligent Design
ISBN-13: 978-0-7660-2911-8

Islam
Understanding the History, Beliefs, and Culture
ISBN-13: 978-0-7660-2686-5

Losing Someone You Love
Dealing With Death and Dying
ISBN-13: 978-0-7660-3067-1

More Than the Blues?
Understanding and Dealing With Depression
ISBN-13: 978-0-7660-3065-7

A Pro/Con Look at Homeland Security
Safety vs. Liberty After 9/11
ISBN-13: 978-0-7660-2914-9

Remembering September 11, 2001
What We Know Now
ISBN-13: 978-0-7660-2931-6

The Scoop on What to Eat
What You Should Know About Diet and Nutrition
ISBN-13: 978-0-7660-3066-4

Sexuality and Teens
What You Should Know About Sex, Abstinence, Birth Control, Pregnancy, and STDs
ISBN-13: 978-0-7660-3312-2

Stressed Out in School?
Learning to Deal With Academic Pressure
ISBN-13: 978-0-7660-3069-5

The Truth About Cancer
Understanding and Fighting a Deadly Disease
ISBN-13: 978-0-7660-3068-8

Unloved and Endangered Animals
What You Can Do
ISBN-13: 978-0-7660-3345-0

Weapons of Mass Destruction
The Threat of Chemical, Biological, and Nuclear Weapons
ISBN-13: 978-0-7660-2685-8

Welcome to America?
A Pro/Con Debate Over Immigration
ISBN-13: 978-0-7660-2912-5

THE IRAQ WAR

A Controversial War in Perspective

ISSUES IN FOCUS TODAY

Mara Miller

Enslow Publishers, Inc.
40 Industrial Road
Box 398
Berkeley Heights, NJ 07922
USA
       http://www.enslow.com

To all those who work toward a more peaceful Iraq

Library of Congress Cataloging-in-Publication Data:

Miller, Mara, 1968–
   The Iraq War : a controversial war in perspective / Mara Miller.
      p. cm. — (Issues in focus today)
   Includes bibliographical references and index.
   Summary: "Examines the war in Iraq from the beginning of the conflict to what it's like to live
there, what it's like for the soldiers, the politics of Iraq, and where we go from here"—Provided by
publisher.
   ISBN 978-0-7660-3488-4
   1. Iraq War, 2003—Juvenile literature. 2. Iraq War, 2003—United States—Juvenile literature.
3. Soldiers—United States—Social conditions—Juvenile literature. 4. Soldiers—Iraq—Social
conditions—Juvenile literature. 5. Iraq War, 2003—Social aspects—Juvenile literature. 6.
Iraq—Politics and government—2003—Juvenile literature. 7. Iraq—Social conditions—21st
century—Juvenile literature. I. Title.
   DS79.763.M56 2010
   956.7044'3—dc22

                                 2009048558

Printed in the United States of America

042010 Lake Book Manufacturing, Inc., Melrose Park, IL

10 9 8 7 6 5 4 3 2 1

Illustration Credits: All photos are from Associated Press, except for the following: Enslow
Publishers, Inc., p. 14; Library of Congress, p. 30; U.S. Air Force photo/Tech. Sgt. Molly Dzitko,
p. 44; U.S. Navy photo/Lt. Joseph Herman, p. 59; U.S. Navy photo/Mass Communication
Specialist 3rd Class Eduardo Zaragoza, p. 87.

Cover Illustrations: U.S. Air Force photo/Staff Sgt. James L. Harper Jr. (large photo);
BananaStock (small inset photo).

C o n t e n t s

Acknowledgments

Thank you to General Montgomery Meigs, Paul Pillar, Colin Kahl, and Staff Sergeant Thomas Zinkle for their interviews and insights, and a special thanks to Dan Byman for being my guide and reviewing the manuscript.

The first Tomahawk missile to be fired into Iraq is launched on March 20, 2003.

The War Begins

At 4:00 A.M. in Baghdad on March 21, 2003, a U.S. deadline passed for Saddam Hussein to give up power. The Iraq War was about to begin. At 5:34 A.M. the first bomb struck. There was a blast and then a wail of air-raid sirens.

It was about an hour before sunrise. Red tracers streaked through the sky. Tomahawk cruise missiles followed. They were aimed at Saddam Hussein's residence in southern Baghdad. Thuds and booms sounded throughout Iraq's capital city.

The attack started sooner than many people expected. Most people thought the United States would wait a few more days before striking. But U.S officials had information about where

Saddam Hussein might be staying. They hoped to shorten the war by killing Saddam in the first strike. Forty missiles and two laser-guided bombs rained down on Saddam's compound. But they did not kill the Iraqi dictator. He was not there.

Anne Garrels watched the attack from a hotel window. She was one of only sixteen American reporters still in the city when the bombing started. It was foggy and she could not see where the bombs were landing. But she could see the Iraqis firing back.

"It woke me up. . . . I heard jets overhead. And then anti-aircraft gunners opened up and sirens wailed."[1]

President George W. Bush addressed the nation forty-five minutes after the attack started.

"On my orders, coalition forces have begun striking selected targets of military importance to undermine Saddam Hussein's ability to wage war." Bush promised to "make every effort to spare innocent civilians from harm." But he warned that the campaign could be "more difficult than some predict."[2]

Not United

Not everyone agreed with Bush's decision to go to war. A CBS poll taken on March 6, 2003, showed that Americans were split about using force against Iraq.[3] "Today, I weep for my country," said Senator Robert C. Byrd of West Virginia to Congress a day before the attack.[4] In October 2002, the U.S. Congress had voted to give President Bush the authority to use military force in Iraq. However, Senator Byrd and others did not believe that the United States should attack a country that was not an immediate threat.

The idea of attacking first against a future threat is called *preemption.* It usually refers to an attack when a threat is imminent (about to happen). For example, it is okay to strike first if there is an army at your border ready to invade.

President Bush believed that Iraq had nuclear, chemical, and biological weapons programs. He wanted to make sure Saddam could not use nuclear weapons against the United States in the future. He also believed that removing Saddam would make the Middle East a safer place and secure U.S. interests.

For the United States, this was a new way of thinking about going to war. For more than a hundred years, the United States had not declared war without being provoked by an attack. Weapons inspectors had not found evidence of nuclear weapons. The Iraq threat was not imminent.

> **The idea of attacking first against a future threat is called *preemption*. It usually refers to an attack when a threat is about to happen.**

Around the world, people protested against going to war. A few people even traveled to Iraq to be human shields. They planned to camp out at possible targets in hopes that it would stop the U.S. bombing. Many of these "human shields" returned home when Saddam Hussein placed them at military sites instead of civilian sites such as hospitals and schools.

There were disagreements within the United Nations (UN) as well. The UN is an organization with representatives from almost all of the countries around the world. It was developed to promote peace and international security. The UN Security Council consists of fifteen members, five of which— the United States, Russia, China, the United Kingdom, and France—are permanently on the Security Council and can veto resolutions they do not favor. In February 2003, a UN Security Council resolution for military action against Iraq failed. It did not go to a vote because France threatened to veto it. France, Germany, and Russia wanted more weapons inspections and increased diplomatic pressure on Iraq. They did not support going to war.

President George W. Bush (on left) shakes hands with Tony Blair, the British prime minister. Great Britain was one of the most important countries to join the "coalition of the willing" in 2003.

However, the United Kingdom agreed with the United States about the need to use force. "If Saddam does not comply, we have to act." said Great Britain's prime minister, Tony Blair.[5]

The United Kingdom would send the second-largest number of troops to Iraq. Spain, Poland, Japan, Australia, and other, smaller countries also signed on and offered troops or aid to help with the operation. President Bush called those who pledged support "the coalition of the willing."

In Iraq

It was hard to know what the Iraqi people thought. Under Saddam Hussein, Iraqis were not free to speak their minds. Government minders traveled with reporters to make sure that nothing bad was said against the government. Some Iraqis praised Saddam. However, it was often unclear whether the praise was given out of loyalty or fear. A few Iraqis quietly criticized Saddam. Most avoided talking to reporters at all.

Saddam also controlled what the media could say. For example, the Iraqi press did not report the deadline that President Bush had set. A few Iraqis illegally owned satellite dishes. They watched news reports from outside Iraq. Then they told others what they had learned. Rumors circulated quickly. But the Iraqi people had no control over what would happen.

There were only thirty-four bomb shelters in Baghdad—not nearly enough for everyone. Some Iraqis left the country, but most were too poor or had nowhere to go. Some Iraqis were afraid to apply for a passport because they might be called traitors and be punished by Saddam.

The Iraqis who stayed did what they could to prepare. They stashed away small amounts of food and water and hunkered down inside their homes. Some dug wells in their gardens. Stores were closed and windows were shuttered.

The evening before the war began, Anne Garrels reported from Baghdad, "The city is strangely quiet. Most people simply shrug, as if to say we are doing what we can."[6]

Military Might

After the failed attack on Saddam Hussein, the bombing increased. Each night, hundreds of cruise missiles hit targets throughout Iraq. People described the attack as "shock and awe." It was a military display meant to show U.S. power. The bombs were called "smart bombs." They were designed to be accurate. Secretary of Defense Donald Rumsfeld explained that the "weapons that are being used today have a degree of precision that no one ever dreamt of in a prior conflict—they didn't exist."[7] The military targeted airstrips, command centers, and communication networks. They also hit presidential sites and places that might have weapons.

Anne Garrels saw a cruise missile "whoosh" by her window in Baghdad. She described the "deafening blasts [that] came one after another exploding into fireballs."[8] At times it looked as if the city was on fire. But Rumsfeld told reporters that Baghdad "was not ablaze. The Iraqi regime was ablaze."[9] The bombs rattled the homes and nerves of Iraqi people. But most of the weapons hit their mark.

On the ground, the 3rd Infantry Division crossed into Iraq from Kuwait, a very small country on Iraq's southern border. They headed toward Baghdad. Their advance would be the fastest sustained military advance in history. A small number of troops entered Iraq through the neighboring countries of Jordan and Saudi Arabia. These troops were from Britain, Poland, and Australia as well as the United States.

Each night, hundreds of cruise missiles hit targes throughout Iraq. People described the attack as "shock and awe."

Special Forces attacked Iraqi airfields and other sites from which the Iraqis could launch missiles aimed at Israel. The United States did not want Israel to get involved in the war. Many Arabs are hostile to Israel. The United States feared that Israel's involvement would inflame the region and make the conflict much worse.

Navy Seals and Marine units tried to take over oil fields before Iraqi defenders could set them on fire. Saddam planned to destroy the fields to prevent the United States from getting the oil. Some oil wells were already burning when coalition forces took control. "Everyone drove in a long single-file column,

Iraqis walk near an oil pipeline in Taji, Iraq. Oil fields and pipelines were the targets of saboteurs opposed to the U.S. invasion.

Embedded Reporters

More than seven hundred reporters went to Iraq alongside the troops. Reporting on war was not new. However, this was the first time that reporters were embedded with the soldiers. The reporters ate, slept, and traveled with the troops. This access allowed the viewing public a much closer look at what was happening in Iraq. But there were restrictions on what a journalist could report. Details about military actions could be described only in general terms. They could not write about possible future missions or about classified weapons. In addition, a commander could declare a "blackout" that would prohibit a journalist from sending his story via satellite. Some people were concerned that living with the soldiers would make it difficult for reporters to be objective or that the reporting would be one-sided favoring the military.

and we did it at night. . . . Our mission was to go and secure the oil fields in the south. . . . You could see the explosions. It looked like a big thunderstorm without the clouds," recalled Thomas Smith, a Navy hospital corpsman.[10] The forces managed to secure the oil fields before there was major damage.

U.S. troops did not know what to expect from the Iraqi Army. The threat of chemical and biological weapons made the soldiers nervous. The troops had trained for those kinds of attacks. They practiced putting on gas masks and chemical suits. Fortunately, those attacks never came. Intelligence reports saying that Iraq's army had these weapons were wrong.

Sandstorms and Oil Fires

On March 24, a sandstorm blew in. It lasted three days. The sky turned an eerie orange color. The wind howled and reached speeds of 60 miles per hour. It kicked up the desert sand and pounded it into everything. The sand got into the equipment. It slowed the troops. It made it impossible for helicopters to fly.

"It was in your eyes, your ears, your nose, your throat," reported Chip Reid, a reporter who was embedded with the 3rd Battalion, 5th Marines.[11]

In Baghdad, Iraqis had filled trenches with oil and set them on fire. The fires produced thick black smoke. The Iraqis hoped the smoke would interfere with the U.S. military's ability to guide the bombs. The smoke did not interfere with guidance systems. However, the sand from the storm combined with the smoke from the fires made the day as dark as night. Then rain came. The sand turned into mud. The mud coated everything.

Even the Iraqis had never seen weather like this. Some Iraqis said it was "God's revenge on the Americans."[12]

Three days later the winds began to die down, and the war continued.

Human Losses

It is a sad truth that during wars, people die.

A maintenance company got lost on Highway 8 near Nasiriyah, a relatively large southern Iraq city with a strategic crossing point over the Euphrates River. The company of thirty-three men and women in eighteen trucks had been separated from the rest of their convoy because of mechanical problems. Most of the soldiers had slept only a few hours in the previous three days. They took a wrong turn. They tried to turn back. But Iraqi forces blocked their exit and fired on them. Eleven soldiers died and seven more were captured. One of the captured soldiers was Private Jessica Lynch.

"It was scary. . . . There was nothing you could do but fire back," Lynch said. "But since my weapon jammed, there was nothing I could do to defend myself. . . . It just felt like it was never going to end."[14] Later, a rescue team freed the captured soldiers.

The Jessica Lynch Story

Private Jessica Lynch after her rescue

Private Jessica Lynch's convoy was attacked in Iraq, and she was injured when her truck crashed. However, the story of the attack was greatly exaggerated in the media. A *Washington Post* article said Lynch "fought fiercely and shot several enemy soldiers . . . firing her weapon until she ran out of ammunition" and that Lynch kept firing "even after she sustained multiple gunshot wounds."[13] This account made Lynch into a national hero. But it was untrue. Lynch had not fired her weapon, and her injuries were not gun related. People accused politicians and the military of inflating the story for political gain. "I am still confused as to why they chose to lie and tried to make me a legend when the real heroics of my fellow soldiers that day were, in fact, legendary," said Lynch, testifying to Congress.[15]

Nasiriyah was also where some of the first heavy fighting occurred. Marine forces were trying to take control of a couple of bridges when Iraqi guerrillas attacked. The guerrilla fighters opened fire and launched rocket-propelled grenades. The Marines had not expected such intense fighting and they were not always sure who was attacking. One Marine said:

> The majority, 90 percent of the people attacking us with weapons, weren't wearing uniforms and therefore you couldn't tell if they were civilian. I briefed my guys by saying, 'If they have a weapon in their hand, they're fair game.' They [were] attacking our position. They weren't just defending their homes, they were firing at us.[16]

Highway 8 would later be nicknamed Ambush Alley because of the number of attacks that happened along that road.

On March 29, a white taxi drove up to a checkpoint near the city of Najaf. Soldiers approached the car to search for weapons. As they got close, the car blew up, killing four U.S. soldiers. Adrian Cavazos remembers the blast. "We fell down and I couldn't hear anything and you couldn't see because of the dust, and then you just see flames flying up in the air."[17]

Highway 8 would later be nicknamed Ambush Alley because of the number of attacks that happened along that road.

It was the first suicide bombing in the Iraq War. A suicide bombing is when a person blows him or herself up in order to attack people or places. It was method of attack that would be repeated many times during the war.

It is hard to know exactly how many Iraqi soldiers and civilians died as a result of the initial U.S. invasion. The chaos of fighting made it difficult to count the number of people killed. Reports by the Iraqi government were not always reliable. Some deaths went unreported by family members. Others may have been reported twice.

The Associated Press reviewed information from sixty hospitals in Iraq. They reported that 3,240 Iraqi civilians had died as a result of the fighting in the first month. "The count is still fragmentary, and the complete toll—if it is ever tallied—is sure to be significantly higher," the report stated.[18] Many civilian deaths happened when power was shut off, hospitals were closed, or there was not enough food as a result of the conflict.

It was not always clear which side was responsible for an attack. For example, on March 26, 2003, a missile landed in a shopping area of Baghdad. Fourteen Iraqi civilians died. The Iraqi officials blamed it on an American missile. But the U.S. military raised the possibility that the missile had been an Iraqi surface-to-air missile that went astray. The Iraqi government claimed the area of the attack was nothing more than a working-class neighborhood. But others pointed to places where there were antiaircraft guns that could have fired the missile or made the neighborhood a target.

Pulling Down the Statue

After three weeks, the battle arrived in Baghdad. "All day long the sounds of rockets, anti-aircraft guns, and artillery presses in from all directions," reported Anne Garrels. "The fog of sand and smoke from fire envelopes the city. Drivers who dare to venture out can't see what's going on just a few yards down the road. Families have no idea how relatives and friends are faring because the phone lines remain cut."[19]

On April 9, coalition forces officially took control of Baghdad. Crowds gathered outside. Some Iraqis greeted the soldiers with cheering. A few threw their shoes at images and statues of the former dictator. This is a very insulting gesture in the Arab world. A huge statue of Saddam Hussein was pulled down with the help of an M88 tank. Some Iraqis attacked the statue's head with sticks and hammers and dragged it through the street.

A U.S. Marine and Iraqi citizens watch as a statue of Saddam Hussein is toppled in downtown Baghdad.

The media sent video images of these celebrations back to the United States. But Garrels reported that many Iraqis seemed "shocked or numb at the events." Some were humiliated by the speed of the defeat.[20]

Dr. Sa'ad Jawad, an Iraqi political scientist, watched sadly as the Marines helped topple the statue of Saddam. He did not like Saddam, but he warned that the American presence would be quickly resented.[21]

Looting

Looters began ransacking presidential palaces and government buildings almost immediately after the troops arrived. At first, they took things that could be easily removed. They carried out computers, refrigerators, office chairs, desks, televisions, and air conditioners. Government cars and large machinery were taken and sold on the black market. Then the looters unbolted and carried out toilets and carpets. They even took the pipes and wiring out of the buildings. Many of the looted buildings were set on fire either to hide the crime or out of anger at Saddam. No firefighters came to put out the flames. The fires raged for days.

Looting also took place at the National Museum of Iraq. The museum held ancient relics from the beginning of civilization. Some of the stolen items were five thousand years old. At the time, museum officials asked some nearby marines to stop the theft. But the soldiers did not have orders to intervene and so they did nothing to stop it. Fortunately, some of the valuable antiquities had been hidden by museum curators before the war began. Other valuable pieces were later recovered or returned. Some are still missing.

U.S. Secretary of Defense Donald Rumsfeld dismissed the chaos. "Stuff happens," he said when asked about the looting. "Freedom's untidy and free people are free to make mistakes and commit crimes and do bad things."[22]

However, the looting was a tragedy. The infrastructure that the "smart" bombing had tried to protect was destroyed by the looters. Infrastructure is the system of public works in a city, such as power, water pipes, sewer systems, roads, and buildings. The Coalition Provisional Authority estimated the cost of the looting at $12 billion.[23]

The looting also showed the Iraqis that nobody was in control and damaged the U.S. image. U.S. forces had not protected Baghdad or established order. They did not seem to care. The

Antiquities looted from the Iraqi National Museum are displayed after their return. Priceless artifacts were stolen after the invasion, but some were recovered.

only building that soldiers had protected was the ministry of oil. Iraqis wondered if oil was the real reason the United States had invaded.

The unrestrained looting also led to increased violence and lawlessness. "Pretty soon [the looting] got into the homes, the neighborhoods, the shops. It then became car-jackings and kidnappings and unstructured crime and organized crime. . . . That was the spark," explained Ambassador Barbara Bodine.[24]

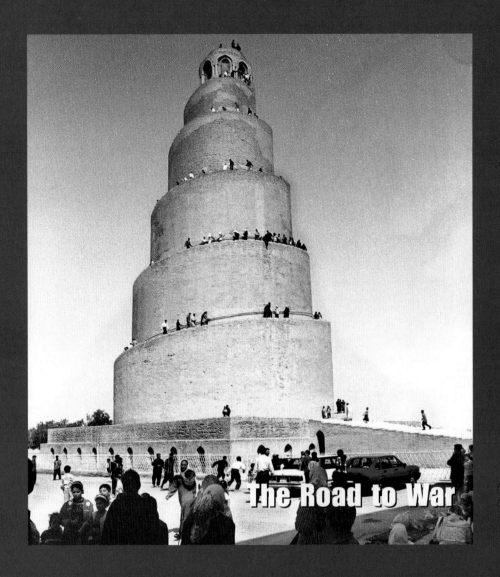

The Road to War

Iraq has roots that reach back to the beginnings of civilization. It is the land where farming and written language began. The area is rich in history. However, in the modern era, the country has never had a strong national identity.

Great Britain drew Iraq's modern borders after World War I. The people within the borders come from different tribes, ethnicities, and religious beliefs. King Faisal described his country in 1932 as having "no Iraqi people inside Iraq . . . only diverse groups with no national sentiments."[1]

There are three major groups of Iraqis. The Shi'a Arabs make up about 55 percent of the population. Most of the

Shi'a live in the southern region of Iraq. The Kurds live in the mountains of northern Iraq near the Turkish border. They make up about 21 percent of the population. The Sunni Arabs constitute about 18.5 percent of the population. They tend to live along the upper regions of the two major rivers in Iraq, the Tigris and the Euphrates, and in the southern city of Basra.

These distinctions are important. After the Iraq War began, fighting broke out between different groups of Iraqi people. The locations of these groups are also important. Iraq's oil wells are located in the southern areas, where many Shi'a live, and in the north, where the Kurds are located. But there is not as much oil where most of the Sunnis live. Iraq's oil is worth a lot of money. The question of how to divide that money increased the conflict between these groups.

Iraq's People

The majority (approximately 78 percent) of Iraq's population is Arab. However, most of Iraq's Arab population falls into two categories divided by religion—Sunni and Shi'a. The original religious divide happened shortly after the Prophet Muhammad's death in 632. The Sunnis wanted a community of Muslims to choose who would succeed Muhammad, while the Shi'a believed that the leadership should stay in the family of the prophet. These divisions led to a bloody war and subsequent conflicts for political power. There are also differences in how the two groups worship. The Shi'a call their leaders Imam. They believe the Imam have a spiritual significance. The Sunni believe it is a sin to attribute these divine qualities to humans.

The Kurds are a different ethnic group with their own language and culture. Most Kurds are Sunni Muslim. However, they never had equal representation in Iraq and suffered tremendously under Saddam Hussein's regime. About 15 to 20 million Kurds populate a mountainous region that includes parts of Iraq, Turkey, Azerbaijan, Syria, and Armenia. Many Kurds seek their own national identity and independence.

Saddam Hussein Rises to Power

Saddam Hussein bullied and murdered his way to power. In 1959, he was a part of a group that tried to kill the Iraqi prime minister, Abdul Karim Qassim. The group was called the Baath Party. They failed in this attempt. But nine years later, the Baathists successfully took over the country's government. The Baath Party was dominated by Sunnis. This meant that the Sunni minority was now in control.

Saddam climbed the power ladder within the Baath Party. Those who opposed him often disappeared through assassinations, mysterious accidents, imprisonment, or exile.[2] In 1979, Saddam Hussein became president. Shortly after, he ordered the death of twenty-two senior members in the Baath Party. He said they were plotting against him. With those men dead, there was no one who could oppose Saddam's rule.

Saddam Hussein was a ruthless leader. He used secret police forces to remove or kill people who were against him. In 1980, he started a war with Iraq's neighboring country, Iran. The war lasted eight years. Hundreds of thousands of soldiers on both sides died. During the war, Saddam Hussein used chemical weapons such as mustard gas against his enemies. Mustard gas is a powerful poison that blisters the skin and causes blindness and death.

In 1988, Saddam used chemical weapons again. This time he used them against the Iraqi Kurds to stop a Kurdish rebellion. Four to five thousand Kurds were killed in the attack.[3] A report by Human Rights Watch quoted a survivor who described how the toxins killed hundreds of victims: "Some 'just dropped dead.' Others 'died of laughing.' Others took a few minutes to die, first 'burning and blistering' or 'coughing up green vomit.'"[4]

Deaths from chemical weapons were only part of the tale. One hundred and eighty thousand Iraqi Kurds are missing and presumed dead because of Saddam's larger campaign against this ethnic group.

Desert Storm: The Gulf War

On August 2, 1990, Saddam Hussein invaded the oil-rich country Kuwait. Together, Iraq and Kuwait hold about one-fifth of the world's oil.

The Iraqi forces quickly overpowered the small country. "I was woken up by a large explosion and I looked out the window and there's the tower all in a pall of smoke," recalled a resident in Kuwait.[5] Kuwaitis also reported abuses and torture by the Iraqis.

The world reacted. President George H. W. Bush declared that the aggression against Kuwait would not stand.[6] The UN authorized the use of force if Iraq did not leave Kuwait. Thirty countries formed a coalition and offered military or financial support to help free Kuwait. The United States military led the coalition into battle.

On January 17, 1991, the coalition forces attacked. It was a moonless night. Apache helicopters began firing missiles at Iraqi forces. Stealth bombers dropped more than two hundred precision bombs on targets in Baghdad. The bombs struck chemical weapons factories and Scud missile plants. Pilots tried not to hit places filled with civilians.

The UN authorized the use of force if Iraq did not leave Kuwait.

The bombing continued for six weeks. After the bombing, ground troops went in. The coalition soldiers were outnumbered. U.S. commanders feared that Iraq would use chemical weapons. They worried that many of the soldiers would die during the assault. However, half of the Iraqi Army had deserted during the bombings. Many of remaining Iraqi troops surrendered without much of a fight.

Shiite women pray at the Abbas Mosque in Karbala. Tensions between Shi'a and Sunni groups threaten Iraq's stability.

"We expected casualties somewhere in the 25 to 30 percent range. But there were essentially no firefights, essentially no battles. The Iraqis were there, but they chose—they elected not to fight," said Colonel John Admire of the U.S. Marines.[7]

Unfinished Business

The military forces successfully freed Kuwait. However, the army did not occupy Iraq and stopped short of removing Saddam Hussein from power.

"You don't do unnecessary killing, if it can be avoided. At some point, you decide you've accomplished your objectives and you stop. We owned Kuwait City. The question was how much additional destruction do we want to inflict upon the Iraqi army that was in the Kuwait theater," explained General Colin Powell.[8] General Powell was the chairman of the Joint Chiefs of Staff during the Gulf War. This is the highest military position and reports directly to the president.

Many people felt that leaving Saddam Hussein in power was a mistake. Saddam used the U.S. withdrawal to claim victory for Iraq. Then he ruthlessly crushed Kurdish and Shi'a uprisings against his government. The United States discovered that Iraq had been trying to develop nuclear weapons. After the war, Iraq's nuclear programs were dismantled. But some people worried that they had been restarted. The United States also learned that Iraq had a secret biological weapons program. The difficulty in discovering this program led to fears that other weapons programs remained hidden.

In 1994, Dick Cheney, secretary of defense during the Gulf War, was asked if it was a mistake to leave Saddam in power. At that time, Cheney said no. "If we had gone to Baghdad we would have been all alone. There wouldn't have been anybody else with us. It would have been a U.S. occupation of Iraq. . . . Once you got to Iraq and took it over and took down Saddam Hussein's government, then what are you going to put in its place? That's a very volatile part of the world. And if you take down the central government in Iraq, you could easily end up seeing pieces of Iraq fly off."

After explaining about the region's divisions, he stated, "It's a quagmire if you . . . try to take over Iraq."[9] A quagmire is a bog or marsh. It is something that is hard to get out of.

Even so, the feeling of unfinished business hung on. Paul Wolfowitz was the undersecretary of defense for policy during the Gulf War. When the war was over, Wolfowitz kept thinking about Iraq. He believed that Saddam was becoming a threat again. In 1997, Wolfowitz wrote an article about overthrowing Saddam Hussein. He argued that the United States should replace Saddam's regime with a democracy. These ideas were not fully embraced by the administration of President Bill Clinton. But they remained in the minds of people who would serve in the next administration.[10] For example, Cheney and Wolfowitz would become major voices in the push for war in Iraq in 2003.

As secretary of defense in 1994, Dick Cheney argued against continuing the war in Iraq. But as George W. Bush's vice president in 2003, he pushed for the invasion.

A man helps a woman who is having trouble breathing after the attacks on the World Trade Center. The 9/11 attacks brought a flurry of legislation in Congress.

The Attacks on 9/11 Changed Everything

In 2000, President George W. Bush was elected to office. He was the son of President George H. W. Bush. Some of the same people who had served under the first President Bush during the Gulf War now served under his son. This included Dick Cheney as vice president, Colin Powell as secretary of state, and Paul Wolfowitz as deputy secretary of defense.

During his campaign, President Bush promised a moderate foreign policy. But attacks on September 11, 2001, changed everything. A group of Islamic terrorists hijacked four planes. They slammed the first two planes into the Twin Towers in New York City. The towers were the main buildings of the World Trade Center. They were a symbol of global and economic strength. The third plane hit the Pentagon in Washington, D.C. It was a symbol of U.S. military might. Brave passengers in the fourth plane tried to gain control of the cockpit. That plane crashed in a field in Pennsylvania. Everyone on the plane died, but the passengers had stopped it from hitting a fourth target.

> During his campaign, President Bush promised a moderate foreign policy. But attacks on September 11, 2001, changed everything.

Fires raged inside the damaged buildings. The two 110-story Twin Towers in New York City fell. Dust and debris darkened the Manhattan sky.

"It is a scene of utter devastation before my eyes," said CBS Radio News Correspondent Pamela McCall as the towers fell. "The second World Trade Center Tower is demolishing. People are screaming in the streets here in utter disbelief, clutching their heads. . . . It resembles the scene of a volcanic eruption. . . . I'm looking down at the site of what used to be the World Trade Center towers. They're both gone."[11]

Altogether, 2,974 innocent civilians died. The attack demanded a response. Almost immediately, people blamed

Osama bin Laden and his terrorist organization, al Qaeda. "The operation looked like al Qaeda, quacked like al Qaeda, seemed like al Qaeda," explained national security adviser Condoleezza Rice.[12] Evidence later proved her right.

There were no connections between 9/11 and Iraq. Al Qaeda was rooted in Afghanistan. But some saw the events on 9/11 as an opportunity to remove Saddam from power. Within forty-eight hours, Donald Rumsfeld, the secretary of defense, was already thinking about Iraq. "We've got to see, somehow, how we could bring Saddam Hussein into this," he told one of his aides.[13]

In President Bush's first State of the Union address after the attack, he said Iraq was part of an "axis of evil," along with Iran and North Korea.[14] In later speeches, he used references to 9/11 to make the case for invading Iraq. For instance, in a radio speech on March 8, 2003, he said:

> The attacks of September the 11, 2001 showed what the enemies of America did with four airplanes. We will not wait to see what terrorists or terror states could do with weapons of mass destruction. We are determined to confront threats wherever they arise. And, as a last resort, we must be willing to use military force. We are doing everything we can to avoid war in Iraq. But if Saddam Hussein does not disarm peacefully, he will be disarmed by force.[15]

As a result of these suggestions, many Americans began connecting the events on 9/11 with Iraq.

The Claim of a Nuclear Program

The Bush administration centered its case for going to war with Iraq on the idea that Saddam Hussein had a nuclear program and that he would use nuclear weapons or sell them to terrorists. The evidence for this claim was questionable. For example, Condoleezza Rice stated in a television interview that Iraq had received a shipment of aluminum tubes that were only really suited for nuclear weapons programs. However, experts in the Department of Energy doubted that those aluminum tubes could be used for that purpose.[16] Similarly, the president claimed in his 2003 State of the Union address that the country of Niger had sold yellowcake uranium to Iraq. Uranium is used in making nuclear weapons. However, the Central Intelligence Agency (CIA) had already determined that the information the president quoted was false.[17]

In addition to nuclear weapons, many politicians and intelligence agents believed that Saddam was hiding chemical and biological weapons. They knew he had chemical weapons during the Gulf War, and they wanted to be sure that those weapons had been destroyed. The UN demanded that the Iraqis provide proof that the weapons programs no longer

Chlorine canisters lie in a defunct chemical plant in Iraq. This plant was given as an example of Saddam's chemical weapons program—evidence that proved to be faulty.

existed. In response, the Iraqis gave the UN twelve thousand pages of documents.

UN weapons inspectors made more than seven hundred inspections of places where weapons might have been made or stored. They talked with the Iraqi scientists. They did not find significant evidence to show that Iraq had nuclear weapons or other weapons of mass destruction (WMDs).

One of the difficulties with looking for weapons of mass destruction in Iraq was the "problem of proving the negative," explained Hans Blix, the top UN weapons inspector. "For example, how can you prove that there is not a tennis ball in this room? Or that there is no anthrax in all of Iraq?"[18]

On February 5, 2003, U.S. Secretary of State General Powell addressed the UN. He presented satellite photos and segments of recorded conversations he said proved that Iraq had a nuclear program. He claimed that Iraq was hiding the evidence before inspectors arrived. However, much of the information that Powell presented was flawed and later proven wrong.[19] Nevertheless, it strengthened the case for going to war.

On March 7, 2003, Blix asked the UN to give weapons inspectors more time to search for the weapons programs that the United States claimed existed. "It will still take some time to verify sites and items, analyze documents, interview relevant persons and draw conclusions," he said.[20] He did not need years, just a few months. But President Bush did not give him time.

The Bush administration knew it would not be able to get a UN resolution authorizing the use of force against Iraq. Instead, the administration argued that Iraq's violations of earlier UN resolutions gave it the right to go to war. Some countries disagreed. They said that the earlier resolutions had not authorized the use of massive force. But on March 17, 2003, President Bush gave Iraq an ultimatum.

"Saddam Hussein and his sons must leave Iraq within 48 hours. Their refusal to do so will result in military conflict, commenced at a time of our choosing."[21]

The decision to act was made. Just over forty-eight hours later, the United States and a handful of allies went to war with Iraq.

People carry looted goods in Baghdad in April 2003.

3   Things Begin to Fall Apart

The invasion of Iraq had been quick. U.S. and coalition forces defeated the Iraqi Army faster than almost anyone had imagined. U.S. news reports showed the images of Iraqis pulling down a huge statue of Saddam Hussein. American support for the war grew. However, new difficulties were just beginning.

The U.S. forces needed to restore electricity and basic services quickly. "We can easily win the fight, but lose the peace," warned retired Army Colonel Johnny Brooks. "If we do not give the people positive signals, and soon, that Iraq is getting better rapidly, and that they have hope, then the gunmen will start appearing and taking shots at U.S. military. Then the suicide bombers will appear."[1] Already, crime was a big problem.

Initially, Jay Garner, a retired lieutenant general, was in charge of administering Iraq and the reconstruction until the United States could organize Iraqis to take over. He watched from Kuwait as looters took over Baghdad. Garner knew that someone needed to take control of the city fast. However, the military refused to let him fly into Iraq for almost two weeks because it was too dangerous.

When Garner finally arrived, he was amazed by the scale of the looting. His team had set up in one of Sadaam's palaces. The place was in shambles. "There [were] no bathrooms. There [was] no running water or anything," recalled Garner.[2]

There was also no clear plan for what was supposed to happen after the military campaign ended. Garner had only had seven weeks to prepare. Arguments with members of the Bush administration over staffing made the preparation even more difficult. Just before Garner got to Iraq, he learned that he would only be there a short time. The Bush administration had chosen a replacement. Former Ambassador L. Paul Bremer would arrive in May. Garner's replacement signaled a shift in policy: The United States now planned to administer Iraq for a longer period rather than quickly hand over control of the country to Iraqis.

Garner tried to reestablish Iraq's government ministries. The ministries were in charge of things such as health, education, agriculture, oil, and electricity. But restarting them after the war was difficult. "Of the 20 [ministries] that we [were] going to use, 17 of those buildings had been destroyed. . . . So if you wanted to start the Ministry of Agriculture again, you had to go out and find another [building], because they didn't have anywhere to come to work," said Garner.[3]

Another problem was that phone lines had been destroyed during the bombing and later looting, so communication had to be conducted in person.

To start the schools, we had to call in the school officials from every major city, call them in, bring them into Baghdad, sit them down in the palace, tell them: "School's going to start on this day. We want you to let them out for their vacation on this day," that type thing. Then you send them all back. And if you change your mind on that, you had to bring them back again. There [was] no way to communicate. It was a manual operation from the day we got there, so it was very slow to get things going.[4]

On May 1, President Bush declared that major combat had ended. He was on an aircraft carrier. A large banner on the ship read "Mission Accomplished." Bush said there was still a lot of rebuilding to do. He promised that troops would stay as long as it took.[5] But there was a feeling that the soldiers would be going home soon. This would not be the case. Violence in Iraq was increasing. There were signs that an insurgency—a revolt against a government or other authority—was starting. Later, Bush's "Mission Accomplished" speech would be widely criticized for being misleading and premature (coming too early).

Bremer's Decisions

Ambassador Bremer arrived in Baghdad on May 12 to take over from Garner. President Bush had selected him because he was a "take charge" kind of guy. Bremer was a diplomat, a counterterrorism expert, and a businessman. He had strong ties to people in the Bush administration but little experience with the Middle East or in nation building. Instead he was known for working long hours and for making quick, firm decisions.

There was a feeling that the soldiers would be going home soon. This would not be the case. Violence in Iraq was increasing.

U.S. and British officials had decided that the Iraqis were not ready to rule themselves. They asked Bremer to lead an interim (short-term) authority until they were. His job was to oversee the occupation and help the Iraqis prepare for self-rule. He worked hard on developing an interim constitution for Iraq. However, some of Bremer's decisions are blamed for making the insurgency worse.

Bremer's first major order was the de-Baathification of Iraqi society. The order said that all full Baath party members in the "top three layers of management in every national government ministry, affiliated corporations and other government institutions (e.g., universities and hospitals)" were to be removed from employment, interviewed, and possibly held for criminal investigation.[6]

The idea was to get rid of Baath party members who committed crimes and were loyal to Saddam or his administration. But the order went too far. It forced tens of thousands of ministry workers, professors, and other professionals out of work and pushed them into hiding.

During Saddam Hussein's reign, many Iraqis had joined the Baath Party to get good jobs, raises, and promotions. "In the past, if you weren't a Baathist, you wouldn't be able to rise in the hierarchy," explained Jabbar Kadhim, a technical director in Iraq's Ministry of Industry.[7]

Between ten thousand and fifteen thousand teachers were fired. Entire schools were left with only one or two teachers. The ministry of education had told teachers to become Baath party members, so they had.

Two workers at a fertilizer plant complained to Tim Carney, an American senior advisor. The men were group members, or *firka,* of the Baath Party. Saddam promoted them to *firka* because they had been captured by Iranian forces and held as prisoners of war for seventeen years. The rank of *firka* offered a monthly bonus of about twenty-five dollars—a fair amount of money for the Iraqis. And they could not turn it down; refusing Saddam Hussein's offer would have meant risking more years in prison. "We are poor and the money is important to us," said

The Most-Wanted Iraqis

In 2003, the U.S. military issued a deck of cards with the names and faces of the most-wanted Iraqis. The deck was designed to help soldiers recognize Iraqis who were wanted for crimes. The highest-ranking cards featured those wanted the most. The ace of spades (the highest card in the deck) pictured Saddam Hussein. The aces of hearts and clubs pictured his sons Uday and Qusay.

Saddam's sons had reputations as bad as Saddam's. They both were involved in ordering and carrying out mass killings. Uday, the elder, was also known for torturing people and raping women.

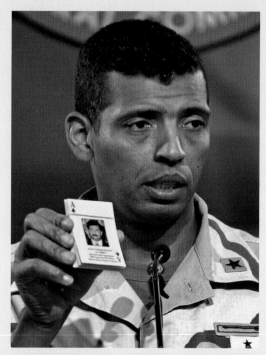

Brigadier General Vincent Brooks shows the pack of cards with the most-wanted members of the Iraqi regime.

On July 22, 2003, the U.S. military learned where the two sons were hiding. U.S. troops surrounded the house. A fire fight broke out between the people inside and the soldiers outside. When it was over, Saddam's sons were dead.

U.S. soldiers found Saddam in December 2003. He was hiding at the bottom of a hole just large enough for a person to lie down in. He seemed confused. His hair and beard were long and shaggy. He did not look like the powerful dictator he had once been.

On October 19, 2005, Saddam went to trial for ordering the killing of 143 Shi'a men in 1982. He was tried in the Iraqi court system. The Iraqi judges found him guilty. They sentenced him to death. Saddam Hussein was hanged on December 31, 2006.

one of the men. "Take the *firka* bonus away, but just let us keep our jobs," said the other. "We are not important people. We are just ordinary men."[8]

Many of the people who were fired were the same people who knew how to make things work in Iraq. Baath party members were often highly educated. They were the managers and workers at the various ministries. If asked, they may have been willing to help the Americans rebuild.

Disbanding the Iraqi Army

Bremer's second order disbanded (broke up) Iraq's army. Many of the Iraqi soldiers had no other way to earn money. They felt disrespected and angry. Some of the former soldiers joined the insurgency.

"The problem you have there is, with that order, you suddenly tell somewhere between 300,000 and 400,000 soldiers that they're out of jobs, and they're all still armed," explained Jay Garner.[9]

The decision surprised many people. Originally, the plan had been to call the army back to help with security and rebuilding. The United States did not have enough troops to do it on their own. It can take as many as twenty soldiers per one thousand citizens to keep a country secure and stop an insurgency.[10] By this standard, the United States needed about four hundred thousand to five hundred thousand soldiers. Only two hundred thousand American soldiers were in Iraq at the time.

"We had too many soldiers to be considered anything but an occupying force. But not enough to actually occupy," said Colin Kahl, a security expert at Georgetown University.[11]

The Insurgency Grows

Violence in Iraq was increasing. Many Sunnis resented the United States because they had benefited from Saddam's rule.

Saddam Hussein sits in court during his trial

Some Sunnis began attacking U.S. soldiers. In addition, foreign terrorists came to Iraq to fight against the United States. They targeted Iraqis and organizations working with the United States as well as U.S. soldiers.

On August 19, 2003, a suicide bomber drove a cement mixer full of explosives into UN headquarters in Baghdad and blew it up. The bomb destroyed the three-story building, killed seventeen people, and wounded at least one hundred more. It was the deadliest attack in UN history. Sergio Vieira de Mello, the United Nations secretary-general's special representative in Iraq, was one of those who died.

"Things just started to fly. . . . I heard an explosion and everything was upside down," said Mahal al-Khatib, a victim of the attack.[12]

When the bomb went off, the UN headquarters had been filled with people trying to provide relief services. They were trying to find ways to repair the country's electrical system, find homes for refugees, and deliver food. After the attack, many relief organizations left because it was too dangerous to stay.

On August 29, a car bomb exploded next to a holy Shiite shrine in the city of Najaf. The explosion killed ninety-five people, including an important Shiite cleric, or religious leader. The bomb left a gaping hole in the street and shattered store-fronts two hundred yards away. No one claimed responsibility for the attack. But this attack and others like it began to set Shi'a and Sunni Iraqis against each other.[13]

By September 2003, attacks on U.S. soldiers averaged more than a dozen a day. Iraqi insurgents placed improvised explosive devices (IEDs) along roadsides or dropped them from highway overpasses. "All of the sudden, the ground in front of you erupts and all you see is shrapnel and cement and fire and smoke," said Sgt. Maj. Bob Metz, describing an IED attack.[14]

IEDs were cheap for Iraqis to make. As war went on, these homemade bombs got more sophisticated, and the insurgents

Soldiers with specially trained dogs search for Iraqi weapons.

got better at hiding them. They put
IEDs into almost anything—soda
cans, plastic bags, and even dead
animals. Insurgents would detonate
them remotely by using hidden wires,
simple timers, and even cell phones.

By September 2003, attacks on U.S. soldiers averaged more than a dozen a day.

In December, a series of four suicide bombings targeted the Shiite holy city of Karbala. The attacks killed thirteen and injured more than a hundred.

In January 2004, a powerful truck bomb blew up outside the American occupation headquarters. No Americans were killed, but twenty people died—mainly Iraqis who were helping the Americans.

In February, suicide blasts in northern Iraq killed fifty-six and injured more than two hundred people.

No Nuclear Weapons

President Bush invaded Iraq based on the belief that Iraq had an active nuclear weapons program and would use weapons of mass destruction. For months after the invasion, military teams searched for evidence of the weapons programs that the president claimed existed. An international team of fourteen hundred people, known as the Iraq Survey Group (ISG), led the search and analyzed the results. They interviewed captured scientists. They searched the scientists' computers. They inspected sites where they thought chemical or biological weapons might be stored. They analyzed materials from laboratories and even tested soil. They did not find any chemical, biological, or nuclear weapons stashes or evidence of significant ongoing programs to develop them.

On January 25, 2004, weapons inspector David Kay said that the Bush administration was wrong in its prewar belief that Iraq had stockpiles of illegal weapons. Kay was in charge of the ISG. Before the war, he strongly believed Iraq had WMDs. But

Hans Blix, the chief UN weapons inspector in Iraq, with UN Secretary-General Kofi Annan

after nine months of looking, he thought otherwise. "I'm personally convinced that there were not large stockpiles of newly produced weapons of mass destruction," said Kay. "We [did not] find the people, the documents or the physical plants that you would expect to find if the production was going on."[15]

Kay resigned. But the search for WMDs continued for almost another year. In October, the ISG released its final report. The report concluded that Saddam Hussein had no chemical weapons, no biological weapons, and no capacity to make nuclear weapons. In January 2005, the Bush administration said the search was over.

Many people wondered why so many experts had been wrong. Former chief UN weapons inspector Hans Blix said that Saddam had been bluffing. "It's like putting up the sign on the door, 'Beware of the Dog.' And you don't have a dog."[16]

Iraqis pass by a U.S. tank in Nasiriyah, Iraq, with their hands up to show they are not hostile.

Living in Iraq

4

Iraqis had mixed feelings about the U.S.-led invasion. Iraqis are proud. Many did not like Saddam, but they also did not like to see the Iraqi Army defeated so quickly. Many felt that U.S. troops needed to stay to help with security and that the United States should help rebuild Iraq. But they also deeply resented the occupation.

In the 1970s, Iraq had been wealthy for a Middle Eastern country. The money from its oil had paid for new power plants, roads, schools, and hospitals. At that time, the education and social services in Iraq were some of the best in the Middle East. Foreign hotels offered visitors luxury rooms with marble-floor bathrooms and rich leather chairs. The city of Baghdad had bustled. People sat at open cafes and shopkeepers were busy with customers.

That was before the Iraq-Iran War, which drained Iraq's treasury. And it was before Iraq invaded Kuwait, which led to the Gulf War and UN sanctions. Sanctions are penalties given by one or more countries to put pressure on another country. In this case, the sanctions banned other countries from trading with Iraq. They were meant to pressure Iraq into following international laws.

The sanctions had devastating effects on Iraq's economy and its people. Wages were cut. Food became limited. Medical care decreased while illiteracy (the inability to read) increased. The UN tried to lessen the effects of the sanctions on the Iraqi people by creating an oil-for-food program. The idea was to let Iraq trade its oil for humanitarian aid. However, the program was corrupt. A UN-appointed panel discovered significant bribery and fraud. About $13.6 billion of oil for food money had gone to Saddam's regime instead of the Iraqi people.[1] In addition, Iraq's infrastructure was not repaired after the Gulf War bombings. Over time it decayed further.

Things had been bad before the coalition forces ousted Saddam in 2003. But now, some things seemed even worse. Saddam's regime had been brutal. But there had been almost no crime. Since the invasion, crime had become widespread in Iraq.

> **The sanctions had devastating effects on Iraq's economy and its people. Wages were cut. Food became limited.**

A young Iraqi woman known online as Riverbend described in her blog how fear and anxiety made it difficult to go to sleep at night:

> After the war, the looting and pillaging kept everyone up. We'd take turns staying up and listening for prowlers or break-ins. My job was always to make the tea. Guns make me very nervous

and I'd stand brewing the tea and eying the gun over the cupboard warily. We'd sit, listening to the radio, the sky . . . waiting for the creak of the gate that would send everyone into a flurry of action— grab the guns, gather the family.[2]

Power Outages

Iraq's electrical system was in disrepair before the war started. Power surges during the bombing had damaged it further. Afterward, looters and saboteurs made things even worse by pulling down cables and electrical towers. Unknown attackers fired a rocket-propelled grenade that blew up a transformer that powered half the city of Fallujah.

Power outages became frequent. In the summer, Iraq can reach 120 degrees Fahrenheit. Without electricity, Iraqis could not run air conditioners to escape the heat. Food could not be refrigerated. The power outages also interfered with the water pumps. This made it difficult for some residents to get water. In some areas of Baghdad, the streets overflowed with sewage.

Riverbend wrote about how simple, daily activities were disrupted:

> The day before yesterday, our area had no electricity almost the whole day. Friday is our "laundry day" so it was doubly frustrating. We stood around looking at the pile of clothes that needed washing. My mother deliberated washing them by hand but I convinced her it would be a bad idea—the water was cold, the weather was miserable and the clothes wouldn't even feel clean. We waited all day for the electricity and once or twice, it flashed on for all of 20 minutes. Finally, at 12 P.M., my mother stated, "Tomorrow, if there's no electricity, we'll wash them by hand. That's that."[3]

Divides Widen

Saddam Hussein had used Iraq's ethnic and sectarian divisions to pit people against one another. He controlled Iraq's Shi'a and Kurd populations with mass killings, imprisonment, and other violent means. He promoted Sunni Muslims, especially those from his hometown of Tikrit and from his tribe. This fostered anger and resentment. Now, with Saddam removed from power, these ethnic divides widened further.

The Sunnis were angry at the Americans. "We were on top of the system. We had dreams. Now we are the losers. We lost our positions, our status, the security of our families, stability. Curse the Americans," said one Sunni Iraqi.[4] Sunnis were worried about what a government dominated by Shiites would mean for them and their families. They were also afraid of the Shi'a backlash against them. Some Shi'a Iraqis were kidnapping Sunnis and killing them for revenge.

Sunni Muslims pray at the al-Imam al A'azam mosque in Baghdad. The mosque became a symbol of resistance to the U.S. occupation and the growth of Shiite power.

The Shi'a were angry at having been repressed by Saddam's government. The discovery of mass graves increased this rage. The graves held skeletons of people put to death by Saddam's regime. The skeletons' arms were lashed together. Bullet holes penetrated the back of the skulls. Some of the graves contained a few dozen bodies, while others contained thousands. Rage over these discoveries increased the number of Shi'a targeting Sunnis for revenge.

The Shi'a also fought among themselves. Leadership of the community was up for grabs. The different Shi'a leaders vied for power. Some of the leaders had ties to Iran. Old rivalries flared up between different Shi'a leaders. Without a strong government, these disagreements often became violent.

Iraq's Kurds mainly wanted control of their territory. Many were hoping for eventual independence. They began reclaiming areas of Iraq that had been Kurdish before Saddam's rule. This was difficult. Under Saddam, Kurds had been forced to leave their homes and neighborhoods. After they left, Arabs had moved into the houses. Now, the Kurds used militias—groups of armed citizens acting like an army—to force the Arabs to leave.

As violence increased between these groups, experts worried that the situation in Iraq could become a civil war.

Moqtada al-Sadr

Moqtada al-Sadr is the son of a famous Shi'a cleric. His father and several relatives were killed by Saddam. Moqtada al-Sadr is not a Shi'a scholar, but his father's reputation helped him launch himself as a leader of the Shi'a.

Sadr's father had started a large social organization. After the U.S. invasion, Sadr, the son, quickly stepped in and revived his father's organization. He delivered food and

As violence increased between these groups, experts worried that the situation in Iraq could become a civil war.

fuel, helped the poor, and provided protection. This increased his popularity among the Shi'a. Some of his followers formed a militia known as the Mahdi army. The militia provided some Iraqis protection but also was responsible for killing other Shi'a leaders and for many revenge killings against Sunni Muslims.

Sadr is charismatic and outspoken. Almost from the beginning, he was very critical of the American occupation.

Al Qaeda in Iraq

Foreign jihadists (Muslims who believe in an extreme form of Islam and fight in religious wars) entered Iraq through neighboring countries. They targeted U.S. forces and Iraqis who helped the Americans. They killed and threatened Iraqis who did not join the insurgency. Through acts of terrorism they increased the civil unrest in the country.

Al Qaeda, the international terrorist organization that attacked the World Trade Center and Pentagon, had not been in Saddam's Iraq before the war. But a branch of the organization was now. Al Qaeda in Iraq was responsible for the attack on the United Nations and the car bomb that killed a cleric

Jihad

Jihad literally means a "striving in the path of God."[5] There are four types of jihad: a jihad of the heart, which is an internal struggle against temptation and sin; a jihad of the tongue, which is concerned with speaking the truth and spreading the word of Islam; a jihad of the hand, which involves fighting injustice; and a jihad of the sword, which involves armed conflict in defense of Islam and is the only type of warfare permissible under Islamic law. The Prophet Muhammad regarded the internal struggle for faith as the greater jihad over the lesser, physical struggles. However, Islamist extremists have used the concept of jihad to call Muslims into armed conflicts and to justify acts of terror. Today, the term *jihad* is often defined as a Muslim holy war.

outside a Shi'a mosque, among other extremely deadly attacks, including many on U.S. soldiers.

Cordon and Sweep

With the violence growing, U.S. commanders tried to counter the insurgency with "cordon-and-sweep" operations. Some military units rounded up as many military-age Iraqi males as they could and sent them to a prison known as Abu Ghraib to be interviewed. The sweeps were indiscriminate. The soldiers did not know if the Iraqi men were friends or enemies, so they took them all. The captured Iraqis were often intimidated, held at gunpoint, and detained sometimes for months.

Thomas Ricks, author of the book *Fiasco,* believes this was one of the biggest mistakes made during the war. Iraqis who may have been neutral toward the United States before the sweeps were more likely to join the insurgency when they came out of Abu Ghraib:

> When you go out and you attack friend and foe and neutral by sweeping them all up, you send a signal: We don't even know who our friends and our enemies are. Then when they get to Abu Ghraib, the interrogators were so overwhelmed by this flood of people coming in that even hard-core people weren't interviewed for 90 days after they were captured.[6]

Abu Ghraib Prison

Abu Ghraib had a bad reputation before the war started. It was the prison where Saddam had tortured and murdered many political prisoners. The name alone brought fear to Iraqis. Now, in a certain Abu Ghraib cell block, Americans were abusing prisoners.

In April 2004, photos of Iraqis stripped naked or hooded and in humiliating positions were shown by the press along with reports of beatings and fear tactics with dogs. "We would

Guards in Abu Ghraib prison intimidate a prisoner with dogs.

bring in military working dogs and use those on the prisoners. Even though it was controlled—like, the dogs were muzzled, they were being held by a handler. But the prisoner didn't know that because he was blindfolded," confessed Anthony Lagouranis, an interrogator at the prison.[7]

The photos outraged people around the world and brought international condemnation. The U.S. Senate met and saw additional photos that had not been shown on TV or in the papers. "What we saw is appalling," said the Senate majority leader, Bill Frist.[8] "American values should win against all others in any war of ideas, and we can't let prisoner abuse tarnish our image," said Senator John McCain.[9]

The abuse fueled hatred and mistrust of the United States. It gave Muslim extremists an excuse for their violence. Shortly

The U.S. Constitution, the Geneva Convention, and the Question of Torture

The U.S. Constitution's eighth amendment makes it illegal to use "cruel and unusual" punishments on U.S. citizens or those in American prisons. The Geneva Convention, a series of international agreements about the treatment of war prisoners, states that "no physical or mental torture, nor any other form of coercion, may be inflicted on prisoners of war to secure from them information of any kind whatever. Prisoners of war who refuse to answer may not be threatened, insulted, or exposed to any unpleasant or disadvantageous treatment of any kind."[10]

After 9/11, the need for information seemed vital for security. The Bush administration loosened the definition of what torture was. They called the terror suspects that were caught in Afghanistan "enemy combatants" and sent many of them to the U.S. Marine base at Guantanamo Bay, Cuba. The Bush administration said that because they were terrorists and not U.S. citizens or members of a legitimate enemy army, the Geneva Convention and U.S. Constitution's safeguards against torture did not apply.

The Geneva Convention does apply to the war in Iraq. However, attitudes from Guantanamo Bay made their way to Iraq. This confusion, along with overcrowding in the prisons, poor training, and vague orders for the guards, led to the abuses in Abu Ghraib.

There are questions about how to balance the need for intelligence with the moral obligation not to torture. The "ticking time bomb" scenario asks what interrogation techniques would be okay if you knew someone had information that could save hundreds of lives but refused to give that information through normal questioning. But this would be an unusual situation. Another question is how much information from tortured victims is reliable. Studies have shown that people will say anything when subjected to intense pain. There is also the risk of torturing innocent people or trying to get information that the tortured victim does not have. Other things to consider are how we would react if Americans were tortured for information and the larger question of whether we can win a war on terror by causing it in others.

after the photos were released, an Islamic Web site posted a video of the beheading of an American in Iraq. The masked man in the video referred to the Abu Ghraib abuses as the reason for killing.

The Bush administration claimed that the abuse was caused by a "few bad apples." Others felt that people further up the military's chain of command should be held responsible. They called for the resignation of Donald Rumsfeld, the secretary of defense. Rumsfeld offered to step down. But President Bush kept him on.

Nine American soldiers were found guilty in the Abu Ghraib abuse case. In addition, Brigadier General Janis Karpinski was found guilty of dereliction of duty and demoted to colonel. She had been in charge of Abu Ghraib and several other detention centers. Colonel Thomas Pappas had been in charge of the military intelligence personnel at Abu Ghraib. He was fined eight thousand dollars as a punishment for two counts of dereliction of duty.

In 2009, President Barack Obama released memos that showed that torture had been discussed and even condoned at the highest level of Bush's administration. The memos gave legal justification for prisoners to be thrown into walls, waterboarded (an act that mimics the feeling of drowning), shackled to the ceiling for hours, deprived of sleep for up to eleven days, and locked in coffin-like boxes.[11] These actions were not specifically meant for prisoners of the Iraq war. However, one memo stated that President Bush was not bound by "international treaty prohibiting torture or by a federal anti-torture law."[12] These memos suggest that responsibility for the torture in Abu Ghraib went beyond the nine military personnel convicted.

Soldiers carry the casket of Corporal Joseph Anzack, killed in 2007.

Soldiers and Sacrifice

By spring 2004, the Iraqis' distrust of the United States had increased. The insurgency was a fact. Tensions were high and violence was on the rise. One of the most violent areas was known as the Sunni Triangle. This area of Iraq is mainly populated by Sunni Arabs and includes parts of Baghdad, Anbar province, and the cities of Ramadi, Samarra, and Fallujah.

U.S. and Iraqi relations in Fallujah had begun badly. Early in the war, a firefight broke out between U.S. soldiers and Iraqi protesters. Several Iraqi civilians died. The soldiers reported that they had been fired on. Others claimed that the soldiers had fired first.

Another incident occurred when soldiers mistakenly fired on Iraqi police. A gunman in a BMW had shot up a police station. The Iraqi police had chased him. They were driving a truck with a machine gun mounted on it. The chase was unsuccessful and the police turned around. A platoon of U.S. soldiers saw the armed truck heading toward them and thought it was a threat. They started firing.

"They kept firing and we kept shouting at them, 'We are police,'" said one of the wounded police recovering at a hospital.[1]

A nearby group of Jordanian police also got involved. In the end, eight Iraqi policemen died. This friendly-fire incident made relations in the area even worse.

Contractors Killed

On March 31, 2004, four American contractors were killed in Fallujah. The U.S. military had hired outside contractors—nonmilitary workers—to run supply lines, provide food and housekeeping services for military bases, and protect U.S. diplomats and generals. The pay for contractors was good. Many contractors were paid between four hundred and six hundred dollars per day. Some even made as much as a thousand dollars per day. This was much more than the U.S. servicemen made, and it caused some resentment among the troops. However, the U.S. military did not have enough people to do the job without the contractors.

The four contractors who were killed were on a mission to pick up kitchen equipment. They were in two unarmored SUVs. The SUVs were brand new and easily spotted. Each SUV was supposed to have three men. But each vehicle was one man short. The teams were missing rear gunners to watch what was happening in back of them.

As the contractors neared the center of town, attackers ambushed them from behind. They shot all four men. Then a mob of Iraqis set the cars on fire. The contractors' burned bodies were later dragged through the street, and two of them were hung from a bridge.

Images of the attack shot by the attackers themselves were broadcast in the United States. Americans were horrified. The military was ordered to invade Fallujah and find the killers. This was not how the military had planned to curb the insurgency. They wanted to use less aggressive raids and to make connections with local leaders to find the insurgents. But the Bush administration wanted action within seventy-two hours.[2]

The First Battle of Fallujah

The operation was called "Vigilant Resolve." Small teams of marines went into Fallujah first. Their mission was to capture

Men from the 22nd Naval Construction Regiment inspect an Iraqi police station in Fallujah that has been damaged by mortar fire.

"high-value" targets. Then about twenty-five hundred marines entered the city. They did not expect to meet organized resistance. But it was waiting.

As the marines entered, they met gunfire, rocket-propelled grenades (RPGs), and roadside bombs. The insurgents were better fighters and better prepared than expected. They fired antiaircraft guns at American helicopters and RPGs at the vehicles. Gunnery Sergeant Nick Popaditch was fighting in a narrow alley when an RPG blew up the hatch of his tank. "I heard a hiss about a split second before it hit me. . . . I saw a bright flash of light and then nothing but blackness. I had been blinded," recalled Popaditch. He later regained some of his vision.[3]

Fighting in an urban area was difficult. Fallujah's streets are narrow and often lined with walls. The houses are built close together. The insurgents knew the area and hid in the houses.

U.S. Marines patrol the town of Fallujah by tank in February 2005.

American forces increased the bombing and gunfire. They were making gains, but at a large civilian cost. Before the war started, Fallujah was home to more than 250,000 Iraqis. During the fighting, it was difficult to know which Iraqis were helping the insurgents and which ones were not. A cameraman from al Jazeera, an Arab news station, filmed the Iraqi casualties and broadcast them. The pictures of the wounded and dead civilians angered Iraqis and the fighting spread to other Sunni areas such as the cities of Samarra and Ramadi.

Bremer began to worry that the fighting was damaging Iraqi support for the American presence. Three Sunni members of Iraq's governing council said they would resign if the coalition did not end the assault. Britain's Prime Minister Tony Blair and others in Washington were also pressuring President Bush to stop the offensive.

On April 9, the United States declared a unilateral cease-fire. Some military officials were angry. "We were relatively close to seizing our final objectives," recalled Colonel John Toolan.[4] Instead the insurgents took control of the city.

Both sides knew a second battle was coming.

> During the fighting in Fallujah, it was difficult to know which Iraqis were helping the insurgents and which ones were not.

The Mahdi Army

Around this same time, violence also erupted in a Shi'a area known as Sadr City. This is an area south of Baghdad where Moqtada al-Sadr and the Mahdi army are located.

Sadr's anti-American newspaper had run the headline "Bremer Follows in the Footsteps of Saddam," and accused Bremer of trying to starve poor Iraqis. Bremer was concerned by the anti-American feelings that Sadr was encouraging. He felt that Sadr was hurting the peace process. Bremer tried to shut down Sadr's newspaper. He also issued a warrant for Sadr's arrest. The plan backfired. Sadr's followers rose up in protest. More than fifty allied forces and hundreds of Iraqis were killed in the fighting that followed. Afterward, several Iraqi cities were taken over by Sadr's militias.[5]

Sadr's militias did not focus their firepower on U.S. forces. Instead, they attacked police stations and government offices. They also threatened the locals who tried to help the coalition. This made it harder for military personnel to make connections with Iraqis who were against the insurgency. Many Iraqis were afraid to even be seen with an American.

The Battle of Samarra

From April through September 2004, several cities in the Sunni Triangle were under insurgent control. Some of the insurgents were foreign jihadists. The military wanted to remove these jihadist fighters and give the control back to Iraqi civilians. They felt they needed a "Sunni Victory" to change the tide of the war.[6] And they needed the victory soon. Iraqi elections were scheduled for January 2005. However, the elections could not take place without more security.

The first assault was in the city of Samarra. Samarra is an ancient city. While its population is mainly Sunni, it is also home to one the most important Shi'a shrines, the Al Askariya Mosque. The mosque is known for its golden dome. It is the burial place of two important Shi'a Imams from the eleventh and twelfth centuries. An Imam is a Muslim spiritual leader who the Shi'a believe is a direct descendant of the prophet Muhammad. The U.S. military would need to be careful not to damage this important religious site.

The operation's code name was Baton Rouge. Troops quietly surrounded the city. To the observer, they appeared to be just another patrol or sweep. But shortly after midnight on October 1, 2004, they struck.

The offensive began with an attack on the neighborhoods around Samarra's edge. "We rolled up on the perimeter . . ." recalled Joseph Hatcher of the 1st Infantry Division. "From there we slowly attempted to move in. We were attacked. We returned fire. We eliminated as many threats as possible."[7]

The military identified insurgents by whether they were armed and firing at the troops. The troops had tried to evacuate the women and children, but it was impossible to avoid civilian deaths. "When you fire a 25mm armor piercing round into a mud hut and it passes through an entire city because there is nothing to stop it, the odds of an accidental casualty are phenomenal," said Hatcher.[8]

U.S. Marine Gunnery Sergeant Joel Pearson hands out newsletters to Iraqi citizens with information on public services. Lack of electricity and other utilities has been a serious problem.

After the major threats were gone, the infantry and the newly reformed Iraqi Army entered and secured the city. By noon, Iraqi security forces were in control of key government and religious sites, including the mosque.

The Second Battle of Fallujah

On November 8, 2004, the military reentered Fallujah. They knew it would be a difficult fight. The insurgents had set up barricades and fighting positions on the edge of the city. Another section of the city had many narrow winding streets and dead ends that were perfect for insurgents to hide in and fight from. The soldiers were told to expect booby-trapped buildings and suicide bombers.

Before the attack, the military warned civilians to leave the city. Most of them did. About half of the insurgents also left the area with the intention of continuing their fight in another area on another day.

On November 8, 2004, the military reentered Fallujah. They knew it would be a difficult fight.

The military began by targeting two strategic bridges with bombs and gunfire. "Jets would fly over the city and drop on strategic places. I think the bombs they were dropping were JDAMs, basically five hundred, one thousand, or two thousand pound bombs onto specific sites that were known to be insurgent-held," recalled Dominick King of the 1st Marine Division.[9] The booms thundered throughout the area. When the bombs hit a weapons cache, the secondary explosions could last more than a half hour.

The soldiers fought their way into Fallujah street by street and house by house. The fighting was intense, close, and personal. The soldiers came up against sniper fire and even faced hand-to-hand combat.

The assault lasted about ten days. During the assault, U.S. troops killed more than a thousand insurgent fighters. Fifty-four American soldiers died. Four hundred and twenty-five Americans were seriously injured. "Where we were in Fallujah, every building had at least [one] bullet hole in it," recalled King.[10] By the end, the U.S. troops had retaken the city.

"Nobody can [say] that they aren't scared. Nobody," said Navy hospital corpsman Paul Rodriguez describing what it is like during battle. "Sometimes you want to say, 'Hey, time-out. Stop bombing us, stop shooting us.' You want to say, 'Stop, cut,' you know? But you can't do that. You can rewind a movie but you can't stop war."[11]

Military Life in Iraq

American soldiers in Iraq joined the military for many different reasons. Some had signed up after the United States was attacked on 9/11. Some had joined in order to pay for college. Some followed a parent's footsteps or joined to better themselves. For others it was what they had always wanted to do. They came from different races and different religions. Sometimes they had differing opinions about the war. But they felt like brothers. And they vowed to protect each other.

"During the train-up for all this, you get to know people really well, and in spite of my political views and my differences with those who served around me, we found a consensus," said Hatcher. "We came to the agreement that in the end, we all want what's best for everyone."[12]

The soldiers worked twelve-hour days, six days a week. Conditions in the camps varied. Most had some form of running water, phones, and Internet, but a few used barrels for latrines. The summer days were hot. The showers were short. "The only way I can describe the heat is, go into a sauna, put it on its highest setting, and feel the heat go into your mouth, and feel it sear your trachea [throat] and your lungs. And that's what you breathe, and you beg for the night to come and let some of the oppressive heat go," recalled Gregory Lutkus, a Connecticut Army National Guard stationed at Al Asad air base.[13]

There was some downtime when soldiers could read and write letters or listen to music. "[We went on] a patrol during the day and then we'd do a patrol during the night. So in between those we could do whatever we wanted, wash our clothes. We even had a TV that got sent out to us which didn't really work all the time because of the sand, but we had magazines and stuff. We had radios; we'd mess around, joke around, and sing a little bit," said Toby Winn of the Echo Company.[14]

The meals soldiers ate while on patrol were called MREs (meals ready to eat). "It was prepackaged food. They're sealed and you can keep them for months. There's all kinds. I had turkey; they had roast beef, and meatloaf, noodles. It wasn't the best," said Winn.[15]

Training and Armor

The training for the soldiers often seemed inadequate. "There were no guidelines about what kind of training we needed for the situation we were going into, nothing about training for certain kinds of checkpoints," said gunner Jonathon Powers of the 1st Armored Division. "We were handed a book about as thick as a wallet, a little green book on Iraq, and that was our knowledge of the country we were about to enter."[16]

Not knowing the language, history, ethnic divisions, and customs caused misunderstandings and problems. Some requests for Sunni areas were routed through Shi'a personnel and never filled. Checklists for evaluating Iraqi police stations were based on American policing standards and asked questions that were irrelevant to conditions in Iraq. Even buying trucks for the Iraqi police could be a problem. "Most people in Iraq drive Toyotas, preferably diesels. Diesel is the easiest fuel to come by. Toyotas are easy to find parts for. The US bought the Iraqi Police full-size, four door, *gasoline,* Chevy trucks. . . . The trucks often sat, due to no fuel being available," recalled Staff Sergeant Thomas Zinkle. "From time to time, [gasoline] would come into a nearby village. The Iraqis would hop in a truck, drive the couple hours to get there, fill their tank, then return to their home village. Typically, it would take over a quarter tank, just to get the fuel. Whenever one of these Chevy trucks had a problem, it simply sat."[17] It was hard for Iraqis to get Chevy parts.

Armor for the vehicles was also a problem. The American Humvee (a wide jeep-like vehicle) was not designed for combat. It was designed primarily as a transport vehicle for personnel and light cargo behind front lines. It had a thin metal skin that was easily pierced. But more than ten thousand Humvees were used in the Iraq War.

> "We were handed a book about as thick as a wallet, a little green book on Iraq, and that was our knowledge of the country we were about to enter."

The Humvees became a favorite target for IED devices. "Every time they got hit, they would fall to pieces," said Winn. "Shrapnel would go through everything and there was nothing to stop the shrapnel from hitting the passengers."[18]

The military sent armor kits to make these vehicles safer. While they waited for the kits, soldiers attached whatever metal they could find to the Humvees. "We'd get scrap metal and then weld it on or they'd get these plates and we'd tie those on the side, they kind of looked like Frankenstein," said Winn. "We'd attach stuff with string and it would start falling off and we'd have to hold it on ourselves. You're holding your weapon in one hand and you're holding the armor by the other."[19]

Personal armor was also a problem. A Pentagon study found that extra body armor could have significantly reduced the number of military deaths in the first two years of the war. The initial armor covered only the front and back of the soldier.

The new armor also protected the sides, shoulders, and more of a soldier's torso. The downside was that the armor's ceramic plates were heavy. Staff Sergeant Zinkle recalls going out on a foot patrol with his men. "When we got back, it was about 4–5 miles, one of my guys went into the gym and weighed himself in his gear. He was carrying 125 pounds!"[20]

Fallen Soldiers

By the end of September 2004, more than a thousand U.S. soldiers had been killed in the Iraq War. And the number was growing. Military men knocked on the doors of the killed soldiers' families to give them the news. "The curtains pull away. They come to the door. And they know. They always know," said Major Steve Beck, a marine whose job is to notify the family. "You can almost see the blood run out of their body and their heart hit the floor. It's not the blood as much as their soul."[21]

Fallen soldiers are buried in the United States with military honors. The casket is draped with the American flag. Honor guards stand at attention. A bugle plays taps. "Everything we do at the graveside is ceremonial slow. Instead of the normal salute and cut—that's what we call it—we hold the salute and bring it back down slowly," explained Joseph Darling, a Marine Corps flag presenter.

> Once they lower the casket into the ground, myself and the other marine begin the flag folding. We each take a spot at the head or the foot of the casket. When I am the one who will present the flag, I stand at the head of the casket because that is where the stars are. The stars with the blue background are always over the heart of the deceased. The stars are always over the heart for love of country.[22]

Military Families at Home

Military families bear much of the burden of a war. The losses and long separations are painful for the parents, spouses,

Sergeant Josh Stineinger kisses his baby daughter, born during his time in Iraq. Military families bear much of a war's burden.

and children of the soldiers. Part of the military's enlistment contract says that military members' service terms can be extended during a war without consent until six months after a war is over. These "stop-loss orders" extended the length of time military members needed to serve. Those in the service had no choice. Some people call the stop-loss orders a backdoor draft. It forced people to remain in the service, even if it was against their will. A few soldiers filed a lawsuit to challenge the policy. "I'm not against the war. This just isn't about that," explained David W. Qualls, a National Guard member whose time in Iraq was involuntarily extended. "This is a matter of fairness. My job was to go over and perform my duties under the contract I signed. But my year is up and it's been up. Now I believe that they should honor their end of the contract."[23] The courts rejected the case.

Some military families faced financial difficulties. During peacetime, reservists and National Guard members are civilians and hold nonmilitary jobs. However, many of these men had been called to service in Iraq. The military incomes were often less than what the reservist or guard member was earning before the war. This made it difficult for some families to pay their bills.

A group of military family members began to speak out against the war. This was unusual. "Military families in history have been pretty much inclined not to do this sort of thing," said historian Michael Beschloss. "It's in a way sort of part of that culture. And the fact that they are doing it now shows how deeply many of them feel about the fact that they were never convinced at the beginning of this war that it was the right thing to do."[24]

"I'm not opposed to war, all war. But what I am opposed to is the irresponsible use of the military, which I believe is what happened in the Iraq war," said military parent Vicky Monk.[25]

Other military family members think that protesting the war is a betrayal of the troops. They believe that the protests hurt the morale (confidence or optimism) of the soldiers. They also think that protests can encourage the enemy. "If my family didn't even support me during the 15 years that I was active duty. . . . That would [have] hurt me emotionally," said Vietnam-era veteran Robert Snyder.[26]

> A group of military family members began to speak out against the war. This was unusual.

The family members who chose to protest believed that they were supporting the soldiers by trying to end the war and bring them home. "How can my wanting to preserve his life and the lives of tens of thousands of others, how could that ever potentially be seen as a betrayal?" asked Stacy Bannerman, the wife of a military man.[27]

Three women display their inkstained fingers, evidence of their having voted in the Iraqi elections in 2005.

The Politics of Iraq 6

Iraq's first democratic elections were scheduled for January 30, 2005. Iraqis would elect a 275-member Transitional National Assembly (TNA). The TNA would then draft a permanent constitution. The representatives would also select Iraq's next president and two vice presidents to make up the presidency council. The presidency council would select a prime minister, who would then choose a cabinet of ministers. "This will be our first step toward joining the free world and being a democracy that Iraqis will be proud of," said Iraq's Interim President Ghazi al-Yawar.[1]

The elections brought fear to Iraq's Sunnis. They were afraid that results would give the Shi'a power and that the Sunni population would not be protected. Two popular Sunni groups told their members to boycott the elections in order to deny them legitimacy. In Sunni areas, the insurgents threatened to "wash" the streets with the blood of anyone who voted.[2] Because of the security fears, the names of the seven thousand candidates were not publicly known until days before the elections.

On election day, around 8 million Iraqis voted in the freest elections ever held in Iraq's history. Iraqis waited in line. When they were done, they dipped their finger in ink so that they could not vote again. Iraqis proudly showed off their ink-stained fingers. There were about three hundred insurgent attacks during the election. But this was fewer than anticipated.[3]

Many people viewed the election as a success. But there was a very big problem. The Sunnis, who make up 20 percent of the population, won less than 2 percent of the available seats. The majority of Sunnis had not voted either because of the boycott or fears of retaliation by the insurgents. They called the elections unlawful. They rejected the results. Most of the insurgency was Sunni. There would not be peace unless all three ethnic groups could work together.

> On election day, around 8 million Iraqis voted in the freest elections ever held in Iraq's history.

The New Government

Like the United States, Iraq's new government has three branches: an executive branch, a judicial branch, and a legislative branch. In Iraq, the executive branch consists of Iraq's presidency council and council of ministers. The council of ministers is led by the prime minister and runs Iraq's ministries, such as the ministries of defense, oil, trade, and electricity.

The judicial branch is designed to make sure the laws follow Iraq's constitution. It is made up of a Supreme Judicial

Council, the Supreme Court, and other courts and offices that determine how the law is applied.

The legislative branch consists of a council of representatives and a Federation Council of representatives from different regions. The elections gave the United Iraqi Alliance (UIA) control of the legislative branch. The UIA is a coalition of Shi'a Arabs. They received 140 seats. The second-most powerful group was the Democratic Patriotic Alliance of Kurdistan. They represented Iraq's Kurdish population in the north. They received 75 seats. The Iraqi List came in third, receiving 40 seats in the TNA. The Iraqi List was made up mainly of secular Shiites. These were Shiites who did not want the government controlled by religion.

The election results were not exactly what the United States had hoped for. The Iraqis did not elect a secular (nonreligious) or pro-Western platform. Instead, the majority of seats went to the UIA, which wanted a religious government and had ties to Iran. The United States was on poor terms with the religiously led Shiite Iranian government. President Bush had even included Iran in his "Axis of Evil" in 2002 when he spoke about the war on terror. The United States also knew that something would have to be done to give representation for the Sunnis.

On April 6, 2005, the 275-member assembly of representatives chose Iraq's new president, Jalal Talabani. Talabani was a member of the Kurdish party. Two vice presidents were also selected, Adel Abdul Mahdi, a Shiite, and Ghazi al-Yawar, a Sunni Arab. These three leaders then chose UIA Shiite leader Ibrahim al-Jaafari as prime minister. In Iraq's government, the prime minister has more power than the president.

A Permanent Constitution

The main job of the TNA was to draft a permanent constitution. The constitution was supposed to be drafted by August

15, 2005. Two months after that, Iraqis were supposed to vote in a national referendum on whether to approve it.

There were several problems to hammer out. The committee drafting the constitution would need to decide the number and locations of Iraq's regions. They would need to figure out how the regions and ethnic communities would divide the wealth from Iraq's oil wells. They would also need to agree on what role Islam would play in the country.

However, before they could start, they needed to resolve the larger problem of Sunni representation. Writing a fair constitution without Sunni involvement would not be possible. Without Sunni participation, experts worried that Iraq might break into a civil war.

After complex negotiations, twenty-five Sunni members were added to the fifty-five-member constitution drafting committee. However, ten of the new Sunni members would not be voting members. By the time the drafting committee was formed, it was July. There were only six weeks before a draft of the constitution was due. And each group—Shi'a, Kurd, and Sunni—had different opinions about the problem areas.

The Violence Worsens

The elections did not lessen the violence. Instead, the number of attacks increased. Insurgents killed more than fifteen hundred Iraqis in the two months after the results were announced. Suicide attacks rose to fifty per month in the first five months of 2005. This was an increase from twenty per month in 2003 and forty-eight per month in 2004. The kidnappings, which had surged in 2004, also continued.[4]

A report released in July 2005 estimated that close to twenty-five thousand civilians had been killed since the beginning of the war. The report attributed 37 percent of the civilian deaths to the U.S.-led forces, which included the bombing at the beginning of the war and the offenses in the Sunni Triangle

Kurds demonstrate with a photo of Iraqi president Jalal Talabani. Differences between the Kurdish, Shi'a, and Sunni groups have prevented the establishment of an effective central government.

and Sadr City. More than 36 percent of civilian deaths were due to the crime wave. Insurgent attacks accounted for 9 percent of civilian deaths. Unknown agents, which included suicide bombers and other terrorist attacks, were responsible for 11 percent of civilian deaths.[5]

Gunmen killed policemen, judges, lawyers, ministry officials, politicians, a mayor, an elected member of the National Assembly, a prison director, and many civilians and children. Suicide bombers detonated their explosives outside of hospitals, Iraqi army and police recruitment centers, checkpoints, and mosques. They attacked near public squares, restaurants, and coffee shops. The attacks even came during religious processions, festivals, and funerals. The roadside bomb was a continual threat to U.S. troops and Iraqi police.[6]

The insurgents who left before the second offensive in Fallujah had reformed in small groups throughout the farm region south of Fallujah. Once again, they were attacking the city. The U.S. military tried to disrupt these insurgent groups.

Religious and ethnic divides split neighborhoods that had once been shared by Shi'a and Sunni alike. "I couldn't open the door and stand in my yard," said Abu Noor, a Shiite living in a Sunni neighborhood. Things had gotten so bad that he and a Sunni friend living in a Shi'a neighborhood decided to trade houses.[7]

Some people claimed that the divisions were made worse by U.S. policies such as the de-Baathification and the elections based on ethnic and religious parties. Some worried that American troops might get "caught in the crossfire between Sunnis and Shiites, Kurds and Turkmen, secularists and believers."[8]

In July, an Egyptian diplomat was killed. He was in Iraq as Egypt's first ambassador to the new Iraqi government. The gunmen hit him in the face with their pistols and forced him into the trunk of his car. The news of his execution came on the same day that two car bombs killed eighteen Iraqis.

Iraqis had good reasons to be afraid of kidnappers and suicide bombers. The attacks were happening in cities and towns across Iraq. For many, these fears were a regular part of daily living. However, on August 31, the fear caused an even greater tragedy.

Shiites were making a pilgrimage to the Al-Kadhimiya Mosque in Baghdad. The Iraqis were on edge. Hours earlier, insurgents had fired mortar rounds near the mosque. As the procession crossed a bridge, a rumor circulated that there was a suicide bomber with a belt of explosives up ahead. The crowd panicked. People trampled and crushed each other as they tried to get out of the crowd. Some were pushed into the Tigris River and drowned. More than 950 people were killed. Hundreds more were injured.

Passing the Constitution

In August 2005, the drafting committee presented a constitution. The constitution proposed a federal system. Iraq would become an alliance of regions with a weak central government.

The Sunnis did not like the draft constitution. "If it passes, there will be an uprising in the streets," said Saleh al-Mutlak, a senior Sunni negotiator.[9] The Sunnis felt that a federal system could lead to the breakup of Iraq. "It's clear from the deliberations about the constitution that it lays the foundation for sectarianism and the division of the country," said a Sunni voter on Al-Arabiya TV.[10]

The Sunnis also worried about the way the oil revenues would be distributed. The constitution called for the natural wealth to be distributed "according to the needs" of the central government and provinces.[11] The Sunnis did not feel that this was an adequate guarantee that the areas that had less oil would receive their fair share of the profits.

Other Sunnis protested the U.S. involvement in writing the constitution. "I don't accept the constitution because it was drafted by America, not by the Iraqi people," said another Sunni voter.[12]

"All the history of Iraq's problems is contained in this constitution —racism, sectarianism and secession," said Hussein Shukur al-Falluji, a Sunni delegate. "If they pass this constitution, then the rebellion will reach its peak."[13]

Compromises

The draft constitution would not pass if a majority of voters were opposed or if two-thirds of voters in any three of Iraq's

An insurgent holds a rocket-propelled grenade launcher in Ramadi, Iraq, in 2005. Insurgents are members of armed groups that oppose the U.S. invasion and the U.S.-backed Iraqi government.

eighteen provinces said no. This meant that in order for the constitution to pass, it would need at least some Sunni support. Last-minute compromises were added to the document in order to get the Sunni vote. One important change was that the constitution could be reexamined after the elections of the new parliament in December. That would allow Sunnis who boycotted the first elections to get a second chance to make changes. Another addition was a statement that simple Baath party membership was not grounds for prosecution and a clause that gave a parliamentary committee oversight of the de-Baathification process. They also added a statement about Iraq's unity and put in a declaration that the official language would be Arabic.

The U.S. ambassador to Iraq, Zalmay Khalilzad, praised the new document. "They have done what only democratic leaders can do—they have discussed, argued, consulted their constituents, and reached compromises," he said.[14]

But was it enough?

More than 78 percent of 9.8 million people voted on October 15. "The two most notable elements in today's voting were, number one, the extraordinarily high turnout amongst Sunni Arabs who had boycotted the elections in January . . . [and] the very low level of violence compared with the January election and, indeed, with the referendum in October," reported John Burns, a reporter covering Iraq.[15]

Ten days after the vote, Iraq announced that the constitution had passed. Two Sunni provinces had rejected it by more than a two-thirds majority. However, in Nineveh, a key swing province in northern Iraq, the "no" votes were only 55 percent. This was below the two-thirds needed to defeat the constitution.

New parliamentary elections were held that December. The Iraqi Accord Front, a Sunni party, picked up forty-four seats in the legislature. It was not enough to make major changes to the new constitution.

Could the War Spread?

On November 9, 2005, an event occurred that made U.S. security experts worry that the war might spread beyond Iraq's borders. Three suicide bombers set off explosives at three different hotels in the country of Jordan. One of the terrorists was at a wedding when he detonated his bomb. "We thought it was fireworks for the wedding but I saw people falling to the ground," said one of the wedding guests. "I saw blood. There were people killed. It was ugly." Fifty-seven people died as a result of the three attacks, and over a hundred more were injured.[16]

Al Qaeda in Iraq claimed responsibility for the attack. This made experts worry that the war might spread. They also worried that Iraq was becoming a new training ground for al Qaeda terrorists.

A different event on February 22, 2006, increased U.S. worries about the possibility of an Iraq civil war. The beautiful golden dome of the Shiite Askariya shrine in Samarra was destroyed. Bombs had been placed in the sacred shrine at night. They exploded at dawn. The bombing came after two days of bloody attacks that had killed dozens of Shiite civilians.

The Shiite community was furious. "If I could find the people who did this, I would cut [them] into pieces," said Abdel Jaleel al-Sudani, an Iraqi who marched in a demonstration protesting the destruction. "I would rather hear of the death of a friend than to hear this news."[17] Shiite revenge attacks hit more than twenty Sunni mosques and killed at least eighteen people including two Sunni clerics.

A different event on February 22, 2006, increased U.S. worries about the possibility of an Iraq civil war. The beautiful golden dome of the Shiite Askariya shrine in Samarra was destroyed.

No one immediately claimed responsibility for the attack. But again, suspicion fell on the terrorist group al Qaeda in Iraq.

"The main aim of these terrorist groups is to drag Iraq into a civil war," said Mowaffak al-Rubaie, Iraq's national security advisor.[18] President Bush promised U.S. help rebuilding the mosque. He urged Iraqis "to exercise restraint in the wake of this tragedy and to pursue justice in accordance with the laws and Constitution of Iraq."[19]

U.S. Public Opinion

Support for the war had been steadily dropping since Saddam Hussein's statue fell in April 2003. By May 2006, President Bush's approval rating was at a new low. Only 31 percent of the Americans polled approved of the job he was doing. Two-thirds said they had little or no confidence that President Bush could successfully end the war.[20]

Midterm elections in the United States were only six months away. The elections were not for the president of the United States, but they could make a difference as to which party was in control of the U.S. Senate and House of Representatives. Since President Bush took office in 2000, the Republican Party had been in control of both houses. Democrats hoped that the disapproval over the war would help them gain seats.

The War's Price Tag

Americans were also upset by how much the war was costing. In 2002, White House economic advisor Lawrence Lindsey estimated the cost of war would be $100 billion to $200 billion. This was much more than the others in the Bush administration wanted to believe. Mitch Daniels, director of the White House budget office, said Lindsey's number was "very, very high,"[21] and Lindsey was fired three months later in part because of his high estimate. In January 2003, Defense Secretary Donald Rumsfeld said that the budget office believed the war would cost less than $50 billion.

Fairly soon after the war began, it was obvious that Rumsfeld's prewar estimates were way too low. Soon the war's cost even surpassed Lindsey's estimate. "I misjudged an important factor," said Lindsey, "how long we would be involved."[22]

By March 2006, the Iraq War was costing $6 billion a month or $200 million per day. Joseph Stiglitz, a Nobel Prize-winning economist, estimated that the cost of the war could reach $1 trillion to $2 trillion.[23] His estimation included indirect costs such as long-term health care and disability costs for wounded veterans.

A Change in Strategy

In November 2006, Americans showed their disapproval over the war, mounting U.S. casualties, and the financial burden it was placing on the United States. They did it with votes. The Democrats took control of both houses in the legislature.

Before the elections, Republicans held 229 seats in the House. The Democrats had 201. Four seats were empty and one seat belonged to an independent. After the elections, the numbers had almost reversed. House Democrats now held 234 seats and the Republicans had 201. The Democrats also took control of the Senate but by a much closer margin, 51 seats to 49.

President Bush recognized the Republicans' defeat as a statement about the war. He said he understood that many Americans had voted "to register their displeasure with the lack of progress" in Iraq and he promised "to find common ground" with the Democrats.[1]

One immediate change was that Donald Rumsfeld was asked to leave his position as secretary of defense. In his place, President Bush appointed Robert Gates. Gates was the president of Texas A&M University, a former CIA member, and the former director of Central Intelligence during the first President Bush's administration. He was respected by both Republicans and Democrats. The Senate quickly confirmed his nomination.

"The next year or two will determine whether the American and Iraqi people and the next president of the U.S. will face a slowly but steadily improving situation in Iraq or . . . the very real risk and possible reality of a regional conflagration [firestorm]," Gates told senators. "I did not want this job. I'm doing it because I love my country."[2]

Tribal Leaders Unite Against Al Qaeda in Iraq

Gates took over command as the violence in Iraq reached new heights. The year 2006 ended with three thousand U.S. soldiers dead since the war began.[3] More than thirty-four thousand Iraqis had been killed during that year alone.[4] The scale of the violence in 2006 was a dramatic increase. Millions of Iraqis had fled their homes. The horrible situation seemed to be getting worse.

Many of the attacks had been carried out by al Qaeda in Iraq (AQI). At first the Sunni insurgency had worked with al Qaeda in Iraq. But AQI's attacks had become too brutal. They began to threaten the power of tribal groups. Not only did al Qaeda attack the Shiites and Shi'a shrines, but they also attacked their Sunni allies who did not agree with them or obey their rules.

In addition, al Qaeda's bombing of the Golden Mosque in Samarra had organized Shi'a militias against the insurgency. The fighting afterwards gave the Sunni a sense of what a civil war might be like. The Shi'a militia had overpowered the Sunni insurgency. A civil war would be long and bloody. The Sunnis also realized that they might not win.

In September 2006, twenty-five of thirty-one tribes in the Sunni-held Anbar province came together and turned against al Qaeda in Iraq. "We held a meeting earlier and agreed to fight those who call themselves mujahadeen," said tribal leader, Sheik Abdul Sattar Buzaigh qaedaRishawi. "Those terrorists claimed that they are fighters working on liberating Iraq, but they turned out to be killers. Now all the people are fed up and have turned against them."[5]

Tribal leaders asked the new Iraqi government and the American troops for support in their fight against al Qaeda in Iraq. U.S. leaders decided to work with the tribal forces rather than against them, as they had in the past. They agreed to pay Iraqis who fought against AQI three hundred dollars a month. With the money, the Iraqis could now honorably support their families. U.S. forces also provided backup if tribal forces found themselves outgunned.

Tribal leaders asked the new Iraqi government and the American troops for support in their fight against al Qaeda in Iraq.

A New General

In January 2007, President Bush replaced General George W. Casey, Jr. Casey was the top military commander in Iraq. He had been in command of the war since June 2004. General David Petraeus took his place. President Bush also replaced General John Abizaid, the head of Central Command, or Centcom. Centcom not only oversaw the war in Iraq but also the war in Afghanistan and other situations in the Middle East.

Admiral William Fallon replaced him. These changes followed the resignation of Donald Rumsfeld. "The idea is to put the whole new team in at roughly the same time, and send some clear messages that we are trying a new approach," explained an unnamed senior administration official.[6]

Petraeus had helped author a new strategy for fighting the war in Iraq. The old war policy focused on transferring power to the Iraqis. The new policy focused on defeating the insurgency. It stressed safeguarding civilians, restoring essential services, and developing local security forces. It also warned against aggressive military raids like the ones carried out at the beginning of the war. In the new plan, small groups of U.S. forces would work with the Iraqis who were against the insurgency. This plan fit well with what the tribal leaders were doing. However, to help the plan work, the United States would need to send more soldiers to Iraq.

Many Americans and representatives in Congress strongly opposed a troop buildup. "Adding more combat troops will only endanger more Americans and stretch our military to the breaking point for no strategic gain," wrote Senate Majority Leader Harry Reid and House Speaker Nancy Pelosi in a letter to the president.[7]

General Casey and several other military commanders also disagreed with the increase. They did not think that more troops could help stabilize the country. In December 2006 a panel of five Republicans and five Democrats known as the Iraq Study Group had advocated for a withdrawal.

President Bush believed the stakes were too high to pull out. He worried that the Middle East could end up in a much larger war and that Iraq could turn into a terrorist training ground. "To step back now would force a collapse of the Iraqi government," he said. "Such a scenario would result in our troops being forced to stay in Iraq even longer, and confront an enemy that is even more lethal."[8]

General David Petraeus speaks with American sailors aboard the aircraft carrier U.S.S. *Nimitz*.

Bush backed a plan to send twenty thousand more U.S. soldiers into combat. The plan also included goals for the Iraqi government, known as benchmarks. Some of the benchmarks included adding eight thousand Iraqi troops and policemen in Baghdad; passing legislation to share oil revenues among Iraq's sects and ethnic groups; and developing and financing a $10 billion program of jobs and reconstruction.

The plan became known as the surge. The term "surge" described the increase in troop strength, but the plan also included the strategy changes and Iraqi benchmarks. General Petraeus believed the surge was the best chance the United States had for improving the situation in Iraq. However, it was still a risk. "We knew that when you do a counter offensive one thing that always happens is that casualties go up," said General Jack Keane, then acting Chief of Staff of the army and one of the strategists for the surge.[9]

The Surge

On January 10, 2007, new troops began arriving in Baghdad. More followed. By June 2007, more than thirty thousand extra soldiers had been deployed.

The military divided Baghdad into nine sections. Each section had an Iraqi army and an Iraqi police battalion devoted to it in addition to the U.S. military troops. "Mini-bases" housed the American and Iraqi forces together. "Previously, our troops had patrolled an area and then withdrawn into large forward operating bases," explained military commander Lieutenant General Raymond T. Odierno. Now, "we moved our troops out into smaller operating bases. . . . These platoon- to company-sized formations lived and slept among the Iraqis, 24 hours, seven days a week."[10]

The Iraqi and U.S. forces worked together and learned from each other. They went on house-to-house searches and cleared areas that the Iraqis identified as al Qaeda safe havens. They built walls around neighborhoods and markets to protect them from extremists. Soon, the Iraqi army and police forces began to take the lead in military operations.

Previously, American soldiers had concentrated on eliminating insurgents and al Qaeda members. These groups were mainly Sunni. Now they treated all extremists alike. If the group conducted unlawful, violent operations, they were targeted. This meant that Shi'a militias and those who carried out revenge killings were also on notice.

American soldiers started patrolling Baghdad neighborhoods on foot. They knocked on doors and tried to get to know the locals. They called it a "soft knock." Sometimes the Iraqis served them sweet tea as a show of hospitality. Before the surge, soldiers had generally patrolled areas in Humvees. "Driving through an area at 30 miles per hour and calling that a patrol is not effective," said Captain Benjamin Morales of the 82nd airborne division. "You're not going to get the information you need. You're never going to establish a rapport."[11]

Because of these efforts, the violence began to decrease. The Iraqis started to feel safer and more protected. More Iraqis came forward to help. They developed neighborhood watches and offered information to root out the extremists. "In 2003, we paid people for intelligence," recalled Morales, who was on his third tour. "Now, people are sick of the insurgents. They're sick of the violence. They're sick of bombs breaking their windows. They'll give the information for free."[12]

The Awakening

Iraq's Awakening movement began with Anbar's tribal leaders uniting against al Qaeda in August 2006. The movement quickly spread beyond Anbar's borders. The groups were sometimes known as the "Sons of Iraq" or "Concerned Local Citizens." By spring 2008, two-thirds of Iraq's provinces had Awakening forces. About ninety-one thousand Iraqi men were

American soldiers in Baghdad ask citizens for help in identifying insurgents. Brought to Iraq as part of the surge, the soldiers are increasing the level of security in the city.

being paid to fight on the side of the U.S.-led coalition. And they were very successful at lessening the violence.

The fighters were primarily Sunni (about 80 percent). This concerned some members of the Shi'a-led government. To calm these fears, U.S. and Iraqi officials required that members provide fingerprints, retinal scans, photographs, and other identification.

It cost the United States around $16 million a month to pay these Iraqi fighters.[13] But that was a tiny fraction of the overall cost of military operations. General Petraeus noted that the savings from the military vehicles that were not being destroyed by IEDs, for instance, "not to mention the priceless lives saved, far outweighed the costs of their monthly contracts."[14] Still, the United States would not pay the salaries forever. Figuring out how to transfer the Awakening forces into Iraqi security forces such as the army and other paying jobs would be yet another challenge the Iraqi government would have to overcome.

Sadr's Cease-fire

Moqtada al-Sadr's Mahdi army was perhaps more of a threat to lasting stability than al Qaeda in Iraq. However in August 2007, al-Sadr ordered the Mahdi army to stop its attacks. The cease-fire came after a bloody battle in Karbala. Shiites had gathered in the city for a religious festival when some Sadrists got into a dispute with the security forces of a rival Shi'a leader. The dispute escalated. More than fifty people were killed, and more than five hundred were injured. The Sadrists were blamed for starting the incident. Afterward, Moqtada al-Sadr directed the Mahdi army to "suspend all its activities for six months until it is restructured in a way that helps honor the principles for which it is formed."[15]

The cease-fire had an immediate effect. According to General Odierno, it was responsible for a 15 to 20 percent decrease in attacks.[16] On February 22, 2008, al-Sadr extended

Blackwater Shootings

On September 16, 2007, security contractors from a U.S. company called Blackwater opened fire on civilians in Nisour Square, an area of Baghdad. The contractors claimed that they were fired on. However, eyewitness accounts said otherwise. "They started shooting randomly at people without any reason," said Ali Khalf Selman, an Iraqi traffic officer at the scene.[17]

Seventeen Iraqis died. An FBI investigation found that at least fourteen of the deaths were unjustified and violated rules about the use of deadly force. The remaining three deaths may have been the result of misperceived threats. For example, a white KIA sedan had been moving toward the security convoy in an area where traffic should have been stopped. The report found no evidence that the Blackwater guards had been shot at.

This was not the first time security contractors had been accused of using excessive force. A State Department report released on October 1, 2007, said that Blackwater guards had engaged in nearly two hundred incidents of gunfire in Iraq since 2005. In most of these cases, "the Blackwater people had fired their weapons from moving vehicles without stopping to count the dead or assist the injured."[18]

The incidents made Americans wonder who was in charge of the contractors. An immunity agreement protected the guards from prosecution in Iraq. They were not members of the military and therefore not subject to military laws. That left U.S. courts. In December 2008, the U.S. Justice Department brought charges against five of the Blackwater guards involved in the shootings. A pact between Iraq and the U.S military beginning in 2009 also ended contractor's immunity from Iraqi prosecution for future incidents.

Demonstrators carry images of Moqtada al-Sadr as they protest the bombing of a shrine in Samarra in 2007. Sadr's call for the Mahdi army to stop its attacks led to an immediate decrease in violence.

his cease-fire for another six months. However, the cease-fire faltered when Iraqi soldiers and police tried to take control of the southern port city of Basra.

Basra is the center of an area rich in oil. It had become a center for smuggling, and Shi'a militias fought for control of the area. This included the Mahdi army, who had had a stronghold in the city. When the Iraqi Army entered Basra, the Mahdi army responded. They blew up one of the Basra's main oil pipelines and gunned down the city's chief of police. Fighting broke out, and the Iraqi Army's offensive stalled.

Sadr's militia was stronger than expected. Clashes spread to other areas, including the poor area of Baghdad known as Sadr City. Iraq's prime minister, Nuri al-Maliki, asked the U.S. military for air support. American F-18 fighter jets dropped cannon rounds on the militia groups attacking the Iraqi forces. During the conflict, more than four hundred people were killed on both sides of the fighting.[19]

On the sixth day, a new cease-fire agreement was brokered between Prime Minister Maliki and Moqtada al-Sadr. The need for American military aid made many people question whether the Iraqi Army was ready to defend the country. However, with the new cease-fire in place and coalition forces helping clear the way, Iraqi troops were able to take control of Basra. Then in May, Iraqi Army troops also took control of Sadr City. This time they did it without the help of the U.S. forces.

Evaluating the Surge

In July 2008, the surge officially ended. The five brigades that had been sent as a part of the troop buildup had left the country. Approximately 150,000 soldiers remained. That was still more soldiers than had been deployed prior to the surge.

People argued about why the decrease in violence occurred. Some said it was primarily because of the increase in troop strength and change in strategy. Others said it was mainly

because of the Awakening movements or Sadr's cease-fire. Some
said it was because mixed Shi'a and
Sunni neighborhoods had become
polarized into all-Shi'a or all-Sunni
neighborhoods making for less ethnic tension. Most experts agreed
that it was a combination of these things.

In July 2008, the surge officially ended. The five brigdes that had been sent as a part of the troop buildup had left the country.

The decrease in violence had enabled the political process
to move forward. It allowed reconstruction projects to begin.
It gave Iraqis a chance to try to heal their divides. None of that
was possible when the violence was at its worst.

"The decline in violence has made politicians more willing
to talk, made it easier for businesses and schools to open, and
otherwise helped Iraqis resume more normal lives," said Dan
Byman, director of the Center for Peace and Security Studies at
Georgetown University.[20]

However, the situation was still fragile. Some people worried that as more U.S. troops left Iraq, the violence would
increase again.

What Next?

It is too early to tell what the legacy of the Iraq War will be. Many questions remain. Will Iraq spiral into a civil war? Or will the various ethnic and religious groups be able to create a working democratic government? Will Iraq become a terrorist haven? Or will a peaceful Iraq help lessen the terrorist threats coming from the region? What will Iraq's relationships be with the United States and with its neighbors Iran and Saudi Arabia? What effect would a democratic Iraq have on the Middle East?

Some U.S. experts believed that Iraq might work best as three different countries based on the Sunni, Shi'a, and

Kurdish regions. They note that the three main groups have in essence developed their own militaries. The Awakening movements were mainly Sunni. The Iraqi Army was mainly Shi'a. The Kurds also have armed militias and already operated independently. Others saw the gains in Iraq as very positive. They believed Iraq could become a model for democracy in the Middle East.

In September 2008, General Petraeus was promoted to the commander of U.S. Central Command. Before he left Iraq, Petraeus addressed the troops and thanked them for their service. "You truly have turned 'hard but not hopeless' into 'still hard, but hopeful,'" he told them.[1] Taking his place was General Odierno. Odierno had been Petraeus's second-in-command during the surge.

Campaigns for President

For most of 2008, Senators Barack Obama and John McCain campaigned for the 2008 presidential election. Each candidate offered very different plans regarding the U.S. involvement in Iraq.

Barack Obama had opposed the war from its beginning. He had also been opposed to the surge. He promised to give the military a new mission—to end the war.

Obama believed he could safely remove the troops from the country by the summer of 2010. "We must be as careful getting out of Iraq as we were careless getting in," he told his supporters.[2] He said he would consult with military commanders on the ground as well as the Iraqi government. Forces would pull out of secure areas first and volatile areas later. He also committed $2 billion toward an international effort to support Iraq's refugees. (Refugees are people forced to leave their country because of war or natural disaster.)

John McCain had supported the war in 2003 and the surge in 2007. He believed it would be a "grave mistake to leave

Barack Obama and John McCain shake hands before a presidential debate in 2008. The two candidates presented very different plans for the Iraq War.

before Al Qaeda in Iraq is defeated and before a competent, trained, and capable Iraqi security force is in place and operating effectively."[3] He called victory the only acceptable exit strategy. While he did not want to keep U.S. troops in Iraq longer than necessary, he pledged to stay in Iraq for "as long as it takes."

As the campaigns debated, another issue became an even bigger concern for Americans. In 2007, a credit crisis developed. The value of houses dropped, while interest rates increased. People could no longer pay their mortgages. The U.S. stock market declined steeply. Banks had to be bailed out with taxpayer money. People worried about losing their jobs, their retirement funds, and their savings for their children's education.

The subject of the U.S. economy became even more important than the debate about the war in Iraq. There was also the question of whether the United States could afford what the Iraq War was costing.

Barack Obama Makes History

On November 4, 2008, Americans elected Barack Obama president. He would be the first African-American president of the United States. His task would not be easy. The United States was entering a terrible economic recession. He would inherit the war in Iraq as well as a war in Afghanistan. The country needed new policies for energy and health care. But Barack Obama had run on a message of hope, and many Americans were optimistic. By electing Obama, Americans said they wanted to end the war sooner rather than later. The question for the president would be how to leave.

> People worried about losing their jobs, their retirement funds, and their savings for their children's education.

On November 27, 2008, the Iraqi parliament also voted to end the U.S. occupation. The Iraqis, in an agreement with the Bush administration, set the date for withdrawal from cities and towns by June 30, 2009. A total U.S. troop withdrawal would occur by the end of 2011. The agreement was needed. A UN mandate that governed the troops in Iraq expired in January 2009. Without a new agreement, the U.S. troops would be in the country illegally. It was time for the Iraqis to decide what was best for their country. A U.S. security pact with Iraq was approved on December 4, 2008. The Iraqis voted 149 to 35 in favor of it. "This is the day of our sovereignty," said Prime Minister Nuri al-Maliki after the agreement was reached.[4] The fate of Iraq was in the hands of the Iraqis.

U.S. and Iraqi representatives sign documents transferring a security station in Sadr City to Iraqi control. President Obama has stated his commitment to withdrawing U.S. combat troops from Iraq by 2010.

Leaving Iraq

In February 2009, President Obama laid out his plan for withdrawing the troops. More than eighty thousand combat troops would leave Iraq by August 2010. Between thirty-five thousand and fifty thousand troops would stay to provide training, basic intelligence, air power, medical care, and logistics. These remaining troops would leave by December 2011. "Let me say this as plainly as I can. By August 31, 2010, our combat mission in Iraq will end," said Obama.[5]

Some people worried that Obama was pulling out of Iraq too soon. They worried that the insurgency would regroup and that Iraq's security forces were not ready. Things had improved, but Iraq was still not safe. In the first six months of 2009, an average of thirteen Iraqis died each day from suicide attacks, car bombs, and gunfire. Still, this was nowhere near the sixty to seventy Iraqis who died per day in 2006 and 2007.[6]

One of the first major tests for Iraq was the U.S. troop pullout from Iraq's cities on June 30, 2009. The Iraqis celebrated the withdrawal with fireworks and parades. President Obama called it "an important milestone" but warned of "difficult days ahead."[7] About 130,000 U.S. troops remained stationed in large bases outside of Iraq's urban areas. But they now needed Iraq's permission to engage in any combat missions.

The last British, Romanian, and Australian soldiers left Iraq at the end of July 2009. The remaining troops were all American. On January 1, 2010, the Multi-National Force-Iraq would officially become United States Force-Iraq. The name change will reflects "the new bilateral relationship between U.S. forces and our Iraqi hosts," said Lt. Col. Mike Stewart.[8]

There were still problems in Iraq and work to be done. Many Iraqis still did not have basic services, such as clean water and decent electricity. Iraq still needed an oil revenue agreement, laws to fight corruption, laws for foreign investment, and rules for political parties. Insurgent groups still tried to provoke sectarian violence by attacks on mosques and religious symbols. But these were Iraq's problems to solve.

Shi'a Imams told their followers to resist the temptation for revenge after attacks. "The sectarian card is an old card and no one is going to play it anymore," said Sheik Khudair al-Allawi.[9] Militia leaders vowed no more spilling of Iraqi blood. Sunni leaders openly condemned attacks against Shi'a.

The Cost of War

Between March 2003 and January 2010, 4,693 U.S. soldiers died in Iraq.[10] Iraqi civilian deaths for this time period were around 100,000[11] (although some estimates are higher). More than 2.7 million Iraqis were displaced (lost their homes) within Iraq. Another 2.5 million became refugees.[12] The United States Congress allocated $747.3 billion to the war in Iraq between 2003 and January 2010.[13] This number does not include additional spending in 2010 and 2011 and any future costs such as medical care for soldiers and veterans wounded in the war.

Only time will tell whether Iraq will become a safe and stable democracy and whether the war was worth the price.

Timeline

1979—Saddam Hussein becomes president of Iraq.

1980—Iraq begins war with Iran.

1988—Saddam Hussein uses chemical weapons against the Kurds in Iraq.

1990—Saddam Hussein invades Kuwait.

1991—Gulf War forces Iraq out of Kuwait but leaves Saddam in power.

September 11, 2001—Islamic terrorists hijack four planes and attack important U.S. sites.

January 29, 2002—President Bush calls Iraq part of an axis of evil.

March 17, 2003—President Bush issues Saddam Hussein an ultimatum to surrender within forty-eight hours or be at war with the United States.

March 21, 2003—Iraq War begins with attack on Saddam Hussein's palace.

April 9, 2003—Coalition forces take control of Baghdad; Saddam's statue is pulled down.

May 1, 2003—President Bush declares major combat over.

May 12, 2003—Ambassador Paul Bremer replaces Jay Garner.

May 16, 2003—Bremer orders de-Baathification.

May 22, 2003—Bremer disbands Iraq's Army.

July 22, 2003—Saddam Hussein's sons are killed in a shoot-out with U.S. troops.

August 19, 2003—Cement truck full of explosives destroys UN Headquarters.

December 14, 2003—Saddam Hussein found at the bottom of a hole by U.S. troops.

January 25, 2004—Weapons inspector David Kay says there are no WMDs in Iraq.

March 31, 2004—Four American contractors killed in Fallujah.

April 4, 2004—Operation Vigilant Resolve, the first battle for Fallujah, begins.

April 4, 2004—First major uprising of the Mahdi army begins.

April 28, 2004—Abu Ghraib prison scandal breaks in U.S. media.

November 8, 2004—Second battle for Fallujah begins.

January 12, 2005—United States officially ends search for WMDs in Iraq.

January 30, 2005—Iraqis vote for a 275-member Transitional National Assembly.

August 31, 2005—More than 950 Iraqis killed after rumor of suicide bomber sends people into a panic.

October 15, 2005—Iraqis vote and pass a new Iraq constitution.

November 9, 2005—Al Qaeda in Iraq bombs three hotels in Jordan.

February 22, 2006—Al Qaeda in Iraq bombs the golden dome of the Shiite Askariya shrine in Samarra.

March 2006—Joseph Stiglitz predicts Iraq War could cost $1 trillion to $2 trillion.

September 2006—Iraq's Awakening movements begin.

November 7, 2006—Americans vote and Democrats take control of House and Senate.

November 8, 2006—Secretary of Defense Donald Rumsfeld resigns.

December 31, 2006—Saddam Hussein hanged.

January 2007—General Petraeus takes command of coalition forces in Iraq.

January 10, 2007—Troop increase and strategy change known as the surge begins.

August 29, 2007—Sadr declares unilateral cease-fire for Mahdi army.

September 16, 2007—Blackwater guards kill civilians in Nisour Square.

July 2008—Surge officially ends.

November 4, 2008—Barack Obama elected president of the United States.

December 4, 2008—Iraq approves security pact with United States that calls for complete troop withdrawal by the end of 2011.

January 31, 2009—Provincial elections held peacefully.

June 30, 2009—U.S. troops pull out of Iraq cities and urban areas.

August 1, 2009—All remaining troops (about 130,000) are American.

August 31, 2010—Deadline for withdrawal of combat troops from Iraq.

December 31, 2011—Deadline for withdrawal of all U.S. troops from Iraq.

Chapter Notes

Chapter 1 The War Begins

1. Steve Inskeep and Anne Garrels, "U.S. Missile Attack Opens War with Iraq," *NPR Morning Edition Report,* March 20, 2003, <http://www.npr.org/templates/story/story.php?storyId=1197440> (August 20, 2009).

2. "President Bush's War Address," *CBS News,* March 19, 2003, <http://www.cbsnews.com/stories/2003/03/19/iraq/main544714.shtml> (August 20, 2009).

3. "Poll: Divided On Iraq," *CBS News,* March 6, 2003, <http://www.cbsnews.com/stories/2003/03/06/opinion/polls/main543034.shtml> (August 20, 2009).

4. "THREATS AND RESPONSES; Senator Deplores Attack on Iraq," *New York Times,* March 20, 2003, <http://query.nytimes.com/gst/fullpage.html?res=9E0DEEDA1031F933A15750C0A9659C8B63> (August 20, 2009).

5. Chris Mclaughlin, "Blair: Iraq's Dirty Tricks Foiled Blix," *Sunday Mirror,* London, UK, February 2, 2003. p. 8.

6. Anne Garrels, "One Baghdad Family's Decision: Stay or Go?" *NPR Weekend Edition,* March 15, 2003, <http://www.npr.org/templates/story/story.php?storyId=1193423> (August 20, 2009).

7. NBC Enterprises, *Operation Iraqi Freedom: 22 Historic Days in Words and Pictures* (Kansas City, Mo.: Andrews McMeel Publishing, 2003), p. 50.

8. Anne Garrels, *Naked in Baghdad* (New York: Picador, 2004), p. 125.

9. NBC Enterprises, p. 50.

10. Trish Wood, *What Was Asked of Us* (New York: Back Bay Books, 2007), p. 7.

11. NBC Enterprises, p. 55.

12. Anne Garrels, *Naked in Baghdad,* p. 136.

13. David Martin, "The Truth And Jessica Lynch" *CBS News Blogs, Couric and Co.,* April 24, 2007, <http://www.cbsnews.com/blogs/2007/04/24/couricandco/entry2723818.shtml> (August 13, 2009).

14. Nancy Gibbs and Richard Stengel, "Jessica Lynch: Oh, God, Help Me Get Through It," *Time Magazine,* November 17, 2003, <http://www.time.com/time/magazine/article/0,9171,1006148,00.html?iid=chix-sphere> (August 20, 2009).

15. Michael Luo, "Panel Hears About Falsehoods in 2 Wartime Incidents," *New York Times,* New York, April 25, 2007, <http://www.nytimes.com/2007/04/25/washington/25army.html> (August 13, 2009).

16. Wood, p. 19.

17. Ibid., p. 31.

18. Associated Press, "Iraqi civilian toll at least 3,240; The count is based on records from 60 of Iraq's 124 hospitals from March 20 to April 20," *Telegraph-Herald,* Dubuque, Iowa, June 11, 2003, p. D.5.

19. Anne Garrels, *Naked in Baghdad,* p. 175.

20. Ibid., p. 190.

21. Ibid.

22. "A NATION AT WAR; Rumsfeld's Words on Iraq: 'There Is Untidiness,'" *New York Times,* New York, April 12, 2003, <http://query.nytimes.com/gst/fullpage.html?res=9E01EFDB153BF931A25757C0A9659C8B63> (September 4, 2009).

23. George Packer, *The Assassins' Gate: America in Iraq* (New York: Farrar, Strauss, & Giroux, 2006), p. 139.

24. "The Lost Year In Iraq," *PBS Frontline,* aired October 17, 2006, transcript at <http://www.pbs.org/wgbh/pages/frontline/yeariniraq/etc/script.html> (September 4, 2009).

Chapter 2 The Road to War

1. Ali Allawi, *The Occupation of Iraq* (New Haven: Yale University Press, 2007), p. 17.

2. Ibid., p. 29.

3. "Timeline: Saddam's Violent Road to Execution," *NPR.org,* December 29, 2006, <http://www.npr.org/templates/story/story.php?storyId=4961744> (June 24, 2009).

4. "Whatever Happened To The Iraqi Kurds?" *Human Rights Watch,* March 11, 1991, http://www.hrw.org/reports/1991/IRAQ913.htm (September 4, 2009).

5. "The Gulf War," *PBS Frontline,* aired January 9, 1996, transcript at <http://www.pbs.org/wgbh/pages/frontline/gulf/script_a.html> (June 24, 2009).

6. Ibid.

7. Ibid.

8. Ibid.

9. Dick Cheney, 1994 interview, *American Enterprise Institute,* n.d., <http://www.youtube.com/watch?v=ZzGGS6GXVIY> (August 13, 2009).

10. George Packer, *The Assassins' Gate* (New York: Farrar, Strauss, & Giroux, 2006), p. 28.

11. Dan Rather, *What We Saw* (Darby, Pa.: Diane Publishing Company, 2002), p. 70.

12. "Bush's War," *PBS Frontline,* aired March 24–25, 2008, transcript at <http://www.pbs.org/wgbh/pages/frontline/bushswar/etc/script.html> (June 24, 2009).

13. Ibid.

14. President George W. Bush, *State of the Union Address,* January 29, 2002, <http://www.whitehouse.gov/news/releases/2002/01/20020129-11.html> (August 13, 2009).

15. President George W. Bush, *War on Terror Radio Address,*

March 8, 2003, <http://www.whitehouse.gov/news/ releases/2003/03/20030308-1.html> (August 13, 2009).

16. Packer, p. 62.

17. Ibid.

18. Bonnie Azab Powell, "U.N. weapons inspector Hans Blix faults Bush administration for lack of 'critical thinking' in Iraq" *UCBerkely News,* March 18, 2004, <http://berkeley. edu/news/media/releases/2004/03/18_blix.shtml> (June 24, 2009).

19. "Powell admits Iraq evidence mistake," *BBC News.com,* April 3, 2004, <http://news.bbc.co.uk/2/hi/middle_east/3596033. stm> (August 18, 2009).

20. "Summaries of Statements Made to the Security Council," United Nations Press Release SC/7682, March 7, 2003, <http://www.un.org/News/Press/docs/2003/sc7682.p2.doc. htm> (June 24, 2009).

21. President George W. Bush, "Saddam Hussein Must Leave Iraq Within 48 Hours: Address to Nation," March 17, 2003, <http://www.whitehouse.gov/news/ releases/2003/03/20030317-7.html> (August 13, 2009).

Chapter 3 Things Begin to Fall Apart

1. Thomas Ricks, *Fiasco* (New York: The Penguin Press, 2006), pp. 134–135.

2. "Key Controversies and Missteps of the Post War Period," *The Lost Year in Iraq,* PBS Frontline, October 17, 2006, <http://www.pbs.org/wgbh/pages/frontline/yeariniraq/ analysis/fuel.html> (June 24, 2009).

3. Ibid.

4. Ibid.

5. President George W. Bush, "Major Combat Operations in Iraq Have Ended," May 1, 2003, <http://www.whitehouse.

gov/news/releases/2003/05/20030501-15.html> (August 13, 2009).

6. "Coalition Provisional Authority Order Number 1: De-Ba'athification of Iraqi Society," May 16, 2003, <http://www.iraqcoalition.org/regulations/20030516_CPAORD_1_De-Ba_athification_of_Iraqi_Society_.pdf> (June 24, 2009).

7. Rajiv Chandrasekaran, *Imperial Life in the Emerald City* (New York: Vintage Books, 2006), p. 54.

8. Ibid., p. 80.

9. "Key Controversies and Missteps of the Post War Period," *The Lost Year in Iraq,* PBS Frontline, October 17, 2006, <http://www.pbs.org/wgbh/pages/frontline/yeariniraq/analysis/fuel.html> (June 24, 2009).

10. James T. Quinlivan, "The Burden of Victory: The Painful Arithmetic of Stability Operations," *RAND Review,* Summer 2003, <http://www.rand.org/publications/randreview/issues/summer2003/burden.html> (September 4, 2009).

11. Author interview with Colin Kahl, Georgetown University, April 8, 2008.

12. Dexter Filkins and Richard A. Oppel Jr., "After The War: Truck Bombing; Huge Suicide Blast Demolishes U.N. Headquarters In Baghdad; Top Aid Officials Among 17 Dead," *New York Times,* New York, August 20, 2003, <http://www.nytimes.com/2003/08/20/international/worldspecial/20IRAQ.html?ex=1221192000&en=0394db3379ac97f5&ei=5070> (June 24, 2009).

13. Neil Macfarquhar and Richard A. Oppel Jr., "After The War: Attack At Shrine; Car Bomb in Iraq Kills 95 at Shiite Mosque," *New York Times,* New York, August 30, 2003, <http://www.nytimes.com/2003/08/30/international/worldspecial/30IRAQ.html?ex=1221192000&en=152549224e62e33d&ei=5070> (June 24, 2009).

14. Eric Schmitt, "The Struggle for Iraq: Resistance; Iraq

Bombings Pose a Mystery U.S. Must Solve," *New York Times,* New York, September 7, 2003, <http://www.nytimes.com/2003/09/07/international/middleeast/07ATTA.html?pagewanted=1&ei=5070&en=56ffffd606de4fa4&ex=1221192000> (June 24, 2009).

15. James Risen, "The Struggle For Iraq: Intelligence; Ex-Inspector Says C.I.A. Missed Disarray in Iraqi Arms Program," *New York Times,* New York, January 26, 2004, <http://www.nytimes.com/2004/01/26/international/middleeast/26KAY.html?pagewanted=1&ei=5070&en=1716a eddc3397c99&ex=1221364I800> (August 18, 2009).

16. "Introduction: Chasing Saddam's Weapons," *PBS Frontline,* January 22, 2004, <http://www.pbs.org/wgbh/pages/frontline/shows/wmd/etc/synopsis.html> (June 24, 2009).

Chapter 4 Living in Iraq

1. "Oil-for-food chief 'took bribes'" *BBC News,* August 8, 2005, <http://news.bbc.co.uk/2/hi/middle_east/4131602.stm> (August 13, 2009).

2. Riverbend, "The Insomniac," January 26, 2004, <http://riverbendblog.blogspot.com/2004_01_01_riverbendblog_archive.html> (August 13, 2009).

3. Ibid.

4. Ali Allawi, *The Occupation of Iraq* (New Haven: Yale University Press, 2007), p. 240.

5. Guy Raz, "The War on the Word 'Jihad,'" *NPR,* October 30, 2006, <http://www.npr.org/templates/story/story.php?storyId=6392989> (August 13, 2009).

6. "Key Controversies and Missteps of the Post War Period," *The Lost Year in Iraq,* PBS Frontline, October 17, 2006, <http://www.pbs.org/wgbh/pages/frontline/yeariniraq/analysis/fuel.html> (June 24, 2009).

7. "Interview Tony Lagouranis," *The Torture Question,* PBS Frontline, October 18, 2005, <http://www.pbs.org/wgbh/pages/frontline/torture/interviews/lagouranis.html> (June 24, 2009).

8. William Branigin, "Senators See Abu Ghraib Prison Photos Held by Defense Department," *Washington Post,* Washington D.C., May 12, 2004, <http://www.washingtonpost.com/wp-dyn/articles/A21551-2004May12.html> (June 24, 2009).

9. "The Torture Question," *PBS Frontline,* aired October 24, 2005, <http://www.pbs.org/wgbh/pages/frontline/torture/etc/script.html> (June 24, 2009).

10. "Geneva Convention Relative to the Treatment of Prisoners of War," *Office of the Commissioner of Human Rights,* <http://www.unhchr.ch/html/menu3/b/91.htm> (June 24, 2009).

11. Dahlia Lithwick, "Have We Softened Up On Torture?" *Newsweek,* April 25, 2009, <http://www.newsweek.com/id/195120> (August 13, 2009).

12. "A Guide to the Memos on Torture," *New York Times,* n.d., <http://www.nytimes.com/ref/international/24MEMO-GUIDE.html?_r=1> (August 13, 2009).

Chapter 5 Soldiers and Sacrifice

1. Thomas Ricks, *Fiasco* (New York: The Penguin Press, 2006), p. 240.

2. Ibid., p. 332.

3. Ibid., p. 334.

4. "Interview Marine Col John Toolan," *Private Warriors,* PBS Frontline, June 21, 2005, <http://www.pbs.org/wgbh/pages/frontline/shows/warriors/interviews/toolan.html> (June 24, 2009).

5. Anne Garrels, *Naked in Baghdad* (New York: Picador, 2004), p. 236.

6. John R.S. Batiste and Paul R. Daniels, "The Fight for Samarra: Full-Spectrum Operations in Modern Warfare," *Military Review,* May-June 2005, <http://usacac.army.mil/CAC/milreview/English/MayJun05/MayJun05/bat.pdf> (August 13, 2009).

7. Trish Wood, *What Was Asked of Us* (New York: Back Bay Books, 2007), p. 123.

8. Ibid., pp. 123–124.

9. Ibid., p. 162.

10. Ibid., p. 163.

11. Ibid., pp. 170–171.

12. Ibid., p. 128.

13. Ibid., pp. 81–82.

14. Ibid., p. 141.

15. Ibid.

16. Ibid., p. 72.

17. Author interview with Thomas Zinkle, e-mail, March 31, 2008.

18. Wood, p. 143.

19. Ibid., pp. 143–144.

20. Author interview with Thomas Zinkle, e-mail, March 31, 2008.

21. Jim Sheeler, "Final Salute," *Rocky Mountain News,* November 11, 2005, <http://www.rockymountainnews.com/news/2005/nov/11/final-salute/> (June 24, 2009).

22. Wood, p. 118.

23. Monica Davey, "8 Soldiers Sue Over Army's Stop-Loss Policy," *New York Times,* New York, December 6, 2004, <http://www.nytimes.com/2004/12/06/national/06soldiers.html> (June 24, 2009).

24. Lee Hochberg, "Homefront Battle," *Online News Hour,* PBS,

October 4, 2004, <http://www.pbs.org/newshour/bb/military/july-dec04/battle_10-04.html> (June 24, 2009).

25. Ibid.

26. Ibid.

27. Ibid.

Chapter 6 The Politics of Iraq

1. "Milestone Elections Begin in Iraq," *CNN.com,* January 30, 2005, <http://www.cnn.com/2005/WORLD/meast/01/29/iraq.main/index.html> (June 24, 2009).

2. Ibid.

3. Kenneth Katzman, "Iraq: Elections, Government, and Constitution," *CRS Report for Congress,* November 20, 2006, <http://fpc.state.gov/documents/organization/76838.pdf> (June 24, 2009).

4. Phyllis Bennis, Erik Leaver, and the IPS Task Force, "The Iraq Quagmire: The Mounting Costs of War and the Case for Bringing Home the Troops," *Foreign Policy in Focus,* August 31, 2005, <http://www.fpif.org/fpiftxt/467> (June 24, 2009).

5. "Iraq Body Count: A Dossier of Civilian Casualties 2003-2005," <http://www.iraqbodycount.org/analysis/reference/pdf/a_dossier_of_civilian_casualties_2003-2005.pdf> (June 24, 2009).

6. "Iraq Timeline 2005," *Council on Foreign Relations,* October 13, 2005, <http://www.cfr.org/publication/8429/> (June 24, 2009).

7. Sabrina Tavernise, "Sectarian Hatred Pulls Apart Iraq's Mixed Towns," *New York Times,* New York, November 20, 2005, <http://www.nytimes.com/2005/11/20/international/middleeast/20sectarian.html?pagewanted=1&sq=iraq%202005&st=cse&scp=116> (June 24, 2009).

8. John F. Burns, "If It's a Civil War, Do We Know It?"

New York Times, New York, July 24, 2005, <http:// www.nytimes.com/2005/07/24/weekinreview/24burns. html?pagewanted=1&sq=iraq%202005&st=cse&scp=107V> (June 24, 2009).

9. Catherine Philip, "Sunnis threaten civil war as Iraq constitution deadline extended," *Times Online,* August 23, 2005, <http://www.timesonline.co.uk/tol/news/world/iraq/ article558089.ece> (June 24, 2009).

10. Lionel Beeher, "Why Sunnis Don't Support Iraq's Constitution," *Council on Foreign Relations,* October 12, 2005, <http://www.cfr.org/publication/9002/why_sunnis_ dont_support_iraqs_constitution.html> (August 13, 2009).

11. Ibid.

12. Ibid.

13. Catherine Philip.

14. "Last-minute compromises on language win broader Sunni Arab support," 2005 Ambassador Speeches, Embassy of the United States, Baghdad, Iraq, October 12, 2005, <http://iraq. usembassy.gov/iraq/101305_compromise.html> (June 24, 2009).

15. Jeffery Brown and John Burns, "Iraq Votes," *Online NewsHour,* December 15, 2005, <http://www.pbs.org/ newshour/bb/middle_east/july-dec05/vote_12-15.html> (June 24, 2009).

16. "Triple Terror at Jordan Hotels," *CBS News,* November 10, 2005, <http://www.cbsnews.com/stories/2005/11/10/world/ main1033309.shtml> (June 24, 2009).

17. Robert F. Worth, "Blast at Shiite Shrine Sets Off Sectarian Fury in Iraq," *New York Times,* New York, February 23, 2006, <http://www.nytimes.com/2006/02/23/international/ middleeast/23iraq.html> (June 24, 2009).

18. Ellen Knickmeyer and K. I. Ibrahim, "Bombing Shatters

Mosque in Iraq," *Washington Post,* Washington, D.C., February 23, 2006, <http://www.washingtonpost.com/wp-dyn/content/article/2006/02/22/AR2006022200454_pf.html> (August 13, 2009).

19. Robert F. Worth.

20. Adam Nagourney and Megan Thee, "Bush's Public Approval at a New Low Point," *New York Times,* New York, May 9, 2006, <http://www.nytimes.com/2006/05/09/washington/09cnd-poll.html> (June 24, 2009).

21. Lee Hudson Teslik, "Iraq, Afghanistan, and the U.S. Economy," *Council on Foreign Relations,* March 11, 2008, <http://www.cfr.org/publication/15404/> (June 24, 2009).

22. Lawrence Lindsey, "What the Iraq War Will Cost the U.S.," *Fortune,* January 11, 2008, <http://money.cnn.com/2008/01/10/news/economy/costofwar.fortune/index.htm> (June 24, 2009).

23. Jamie Wilson, "Iraq War Could Cost U.S. Over $2 Trillion, says Nobel Prize-Winning Economist," *The Guardian,* January 7, 2006, <http://www.guardian.co.uk/world/2006/jan/07/usa.iraq> (June 24, 2009).

Chapter 7 A Change in Strategy

1. "In Full, President Bush's Speech," *BBC News,* November 8, 2006, <http://news.bbc.co.uk/2/hi/americas/6131740.stm> (January 31, 2010).

2. "U.S. 'Not Winning Conflict in Iraq,'" *BBC News,* December 5, 2006, <http://news.bbc.co.uk/2/hi/world/americas/6209356.stm> (June 24, 2009).

3. Lizette Alvarez and Andrew Lehren, "3,000 Deaths in Iraq, Countless Tears at Home," *New York Times,* New York, January 1, 2007, <http://www.nytimes.com/2007/01/01/us/01deaths.html> (June 24, 2009).

4. Sabrina Tavernise, "Iraqi Death Toll Exceeded 34,000 in 2006, U.N. Says," *New York Times,* New York, January 17, 2007, <http://www.nytimes.com/2007/01/17/world/middleeast/17iraq.html> (June 24, 2009).

5. Khalid Al-Ansary and Ali Adeeb, "Most Tribes in Anbar Agree to Unite Against Insurgents," *New York Times,* New York, September 18, 2006, <http://www.nytimes.com/2006/09/18/world/middleeast/18iraq.html> (June 24, 2009).

6. Michael Gordon and Thom Shanker, "Bush to Name a New General to Oversee Iraq," *New York Times,* New York, January 5, 2007, <http://www.nytimes.com/2007/01/05/world/middleeast/05military.html> (June 24, 2009).

7. "Congressional Leaders Call on President to Reject Flawed Iraq Troop Surge," *Speaker Nancy Pelosi Web Site,* January 5, 2007, <http://www.speaker.gov/newsroom/pressreleases?id=0021> (September 8, 2009).

8. David E. Sanger, "Bush Adds Troops in Bid to Secure Iraq," *New York Times,* New York, January 11, 2007, <http://www.nytimes.com/2007/01/11/world/middleeast/11prexy.html> (August 13, 2009).

9. "Is Surge Responsible for a Less Violent Iraq?" *Morning Edition, NPR,* September 26, 2008, <http://www.npr.org/templates/player/mediaPlayer.html?action=1&t=1&islist=false&id=95076165&m=95076141> (August 13, 2009).

10. "2007 Surge of Ground Forces in Iraq—Risks, Challenges and Successes: An Interview with Lieutenant General Raymond T. Odierno," *Fires,* March-April 2008, <http://sill-www.army.mil/firesbulletin/2008/Mar_Apr_2008/Mar_Apr_2008.pdf> (August 13, 2009).

11. Edward Wong, "Iraq Plan's Elusive Target: Fear Itself," *New York Times,* New York, April 8, 2007, <http://www.nytimes.

com/2007/04/08/weekinreview/08wong.html> (June 24, 2009).

12. Ibid.

13. Greg Bruno, "The Role of the 'Sons of Iraq' in Improving Security," *Council on Foreign Relations,* April 25, 2008, <http://www.cfr.org/publication/16088/> (June 24, 2009).

14. CQ Transcripts, "Gen. Petraeus's Opening Remarks on Iraq," *Washington Post,* Washington, D.C., April 8, 2008, <http://www.washingtonpost.com/wp-dyn/content/ article/2008/04/08/AR2008040801363_pf.html> (June 24, 2009).

15. Damien McElroy, "Moqtada al-Sadr announces ceasefire in Iraq," *Telegraph.co.uk,* London, England, August 30, 2007, <http://www.telegraph.co.uk/news/worldnews/1561731/ Moqtada-al-Sadr-announces-ceasefire-in-Iraq.html> (June 24, 2009).

16. Mark Kukis, "Al-Sadr's Fragile Peace," *Time,* February 20, 2008, <http://www.time.com/time/world/ article/0,8599,1714848,00.html> (June 24, 2009).

17. Ginger Thompson and Katherine Zoepf, "Lawyers Say U.S. Reckless in Charges for 5 Guards," *New York Times,* New York, December 6, 2008, <http://www.nytimes. com/2008/12/07/world/middleeast/07iraq.html> (August 13, 2009).

18. David Stout and John M. Broder, "Report Depicts Recklessness at Blackwater," *New York Times,* New York, October 1, 2007, <http://www.nytimes.com/2007/10/01/ washington/01cnd-blackwater.html> (June 24, 2009).

19. Sudarsan Raghavan and Sholnn Freeman, "U.S. Appears to Take Lead in Fighting in Baghdad," *Washington Post,* Washington, D.C., April 1, 2008, <http://www. washingtonpost.com/wp-dyn/content/article/2008/04/01/ AR2008040100833.html> (June 24, 2009).

20. Author interview with Dan Byman, e-mail, November 30, 2008.

Chapter 8 What Next?

1. Julie E. Barnes and Tina Susman, "Gen. Ray Odierno takes over for Petraeus in Iraq," *Los Angeles Times,* Los Angeles, September 17, 2008, <http://articles.latimes.com/2008/sep/17/world/fg-iraq17> (June 24, 2009).

2. Barack Obama, "My Plan for Iraq," *New York Times,* New York, July 14, 2008, <http://www.nytimes.com/2008/07/14/opinion/14obama.html> (June 24, 2009).

3. "Strategy for Victory in Iraq," *McCain-Palin Web site,* <http://www.johnmccain.com/Informing/Issues/fdeb03a7-30b0-4ece-8e34-4c7ea83f11d8.htm> (November 1, 2008).

4. Alissa Rubin and Campbell Robertson, "Iraq Backs Deal That Sets End of U.S. Role," *New York Times,* New York, November 27, 2008, <http://www.nytimes.com/2008/11/28/world/middleeast/28iraq.html> (June 24, 2009).

5. Peter Baker, "With Pledges to Troops and Iraqis Obama Details Pullout," *New York Times,* New York, February 26, 2009, <http://www.nytimes.com/2009/02/28/washington/28troops.html> (August 13, 2009).

6. "Documented Civilian Deaths from Violence," *Iraq Body Count,* n.d., <http://www.iraqbodycount.org/database/> (August 13, 2009).

7. Alissa Rubin, "Iraq Marks Withdrawal of U.S. Troops from Cities," *New York Times,* New York, June 30, 2009, <http://www.nytimes.com/2009/07/01/world/middleeast/01iraq.html> (August 13, 2009).

8. Rod Nordland and Timothy Williams, "Iraq force soon to be a coalition of one," *New York Times,* New York, July 28, 2009, <http://www.nytimes.com/2009/07/29/world/middleeast/29iraq.html> (August 13, 2009).

9. Rod Nordland, "Iraq shiites show restraint after attacks," *New York Times,* New York, August 11, 2009, <http://www.nytimes.com/2009/08/12/world/middleeast/12shiite.html?hp> (August 13, 2009).

10. "Iraq Coalition Casualty Count," *icasualties.org,* <http://icasualties.org/Iraq/index.aspx> (January 31, 2010).

11. Iraq Body Count.

12. Brookings Institute, "Iraq Index," July 25, 2009, <http://www.brookings.edu/saban/~/media/Files/Centers/Saban/Iraq%20Index/index20090625.pdf> (August 13, 2009).

13. National Priorities Project, "Notes and Sources: Cost of War Counter," n.d., <http://www.nationalpriorities.org/cost_of_war_counter_notes> (January 31, 2010).

Glossary

al Qaeda—An international terrorist organization.

ambush—An unexpected attack.

assassination—The killing of a political leader or public figure.

axis—An association of groups that forms a center of power.

barricades—Barriers that block a route.

cache—A hidden supply of something, such as weapons or valuables.

casualty—Someone who is killed or injured during combat.

charismatic—Having charm or influence.

civil war—A war between groups existing within a country.

civilian—Someone who is not a member of the armed forces.

cleric—A religious leader.

coalition—A temporary union between groups, countries, or political parties.

condemnation—Strong disapproval.

cordon—The act of surrounding an area to control access to and from it.

demote—Lose rank, status, or position.

dereliction—Neglect of duty.

detention—The act of keeping someone in custody.

extremist—Someone with extreme views who uses methods way beyond the norm.

fragmentary—Consisting of disconnected items.

friendly fire—Gun or artillery fire not from an enemy.

guerrillas—Members of a small armed force that fight a stronger force by sabotage.

immunity—Freedom from prosecution or punishment.

indiscriminate—Without considering differences.

infantry—Foot soldiers.

infrastructure—Public systems, services, and facilities of a country.

insurgency—A revolt or uprising.

interrogator—Someone who aggressively questions a person.

invasion—A hostile entry into a country by an armed force.

jihad—A struggle in the name of God, often used to refer to a holy war.

jihadist—Muslims who believe in an extreme form of Islam and fight in religious wars.

latrines—Toilets.

legacy—Something handed down from a previous generation or time.

legitimacy—Legal standing.

militia—A group of civilians who are armed and act as an army.

mujahedin—A jihadist or Muslim guerrilla warrior.

occupation—Control of a nation by foreign armed forces.

offensive—An attack or assault.

precision—Exactness or accuracy.

rapport—A friendly relationship.

referendum—A vote on a specific question.

regime—A controlling group or government usually considered harsh or cruel.

revenge—Something done to get even with somebody who has caused harm.

saboteur—Somebody who deliberately damages property or equipment.

sanction—A penalty imposed for breaking a rule.

sectarianism—Strong and often narrow-minded support for one sect or party.

shrapnel—Fragments that are scattered when a shell, bomb, or bullet explodes.

suicide bombing—A bombing in which the bomber dies in the explosion.

ultimatum—A demand that includes a threat if the demand is not followed.

unilateral—Decided and acted on by one side or group.

Further Reading

Arnold, James R. *Saddam Hussein's Iraq.* Minneapolis: Twenty-First Century Books, 2009.

Lansford, Tom, ed. *The War in Iraq.* Detroit: Greenhaven Press, 2009.

Peterson, J. E. *Tensions in the Gulf, 1978–1991.* Philadelphia: Mason Crest Publishers, 2007.

Silverstein, Adam J. *Islamic History: A Very Short Introduction.* New York: Oxford University Press USA, 2010.

Smithson, Ryan. *Ghosts of War: The True Story of a 19-Year-Old GI.* New York: HarperCollins, 2009.

Wagner, Heather Lehr. *Iraq.* New York: Chelsea House, 2009.

Internet Addresses

The New York Times: Iraq
<http://topics.nytimes.com/topics/news/international/countriesandterritories/iraq/>

Online Newshour: Iraq in Transition
<http://www.pbs.org/newshour/indepth_coverage/middle_east/iraq/>

Index